Salad Days

LOVE FOOD™

This edition published by Parragon Books Ltd in 2014
and distributed by

Parragon Inc.
440 Park Avenue South, 13th Floor
New York, NY 10016
www.parragon.com/lovefood

LOVE FOOD is an imprint of Parragon Books Ltd

ISBN 978-1-4723-4101-3

Printed in China

Created and produced by Pene Parker and Becca Spry
New recipes and food styling: Sara Lewis
Photographer: Haraala Hamilton

Notes for the reader
This book uses standard kitchen measuring spoons and cups. All spoon
and cup measurements are level unless otherwise indicated. Unless
otherwise stated, milk is assumed to be whole, eggs are large, individual
vegetables are medium, pepper is freshly ground black pepper and all
root vegetables should be peeled prior to use. Garnishes, decorations, and
serving suggestions are all optional and not necessarily included in the
recipe ingredients or method. Any optional ingredients and seasoning
to taste are not included in the nutritional analysis. While the author has
made all reasonable efforts to ensure that the information contained
in this book is accurate and up to date at the time of publication, anyone
reading this book should note the following important points:-

• Medical and pharmaceutical knowledge is constantly changing and the
author and the publisher cannot and do not guarantee the accuracy or
appropriateness of the contents of this book;

• In any event, this book is not intended to be, and should not be relied
upon, as a substitute for advice from your healthcare practitioner, or
any other healthcare professional. You should consult a healthcare
practitioner before making any major dietary changes;

• Food Allergy Disclaimer: The author and the publisher are not
responsible for any adverse reactions to the recipes contained herein.

• The statements in this book have not been evaluated by the U.S. Food and
Drug Administration. This book is not intended to treat, cure or prevent
any disease.

• For the reasons set out above, and to the fullest extent permitted by law,
the author and the publisher: (i) cannot and do not accept any legal duty
of care or responsibility in relation to the accuracy or appropriateness of
the contents of this book, even where expressed as "advice" or using other
words to this effect; and (ii) disclaim any liability, loss, damage or risk that
may be claimed or incurred as a consequence - directly or indirectly - of
the use and/or application of any of the contents of this book.

Salad Days

Salads have come a long way from the simple lettuce, tomato, and cucumber-base meals our mothers used to serve. Foreign vacations have inspired a passion for culinary exploration, and with so many exciting ingredients now available in the stores, we can recreate salads from all over the world and experiment with new ideas.

Salads combine a variety of textures, with delicate lettuce leaves contrasting, for instance, with crunchy celery, radishes, seeds, and nuts, and creamy avocado or Brie. Often salads mix up tastes, too, with salty feta cheese sharing a plate with peppery arugula, or bitter radicchio flavored with sweet aged balsamic vinegar.

The key to a healthy diet

Nutritionists agree that the key to a healthy diet is variety. Eating more vegetables and fruit can help you look good and feel great and give you plenty of energy. It can also help to prevent some cancers and lower the risk of coronary heart disease, diabetes, and certain digestive problems.

It is recommended that we should aim to eat at least five portions of vegetables and fruit each day and reduce our consumption of meat, fat, and sugary foods. Eating more salads is an excellent way to achieve this.

Most ingredients in a salad are served raw or lightly cooked, which means the nutrient levels are at their optimum. Raw foods tend to need more chewing than cooked foods and take longer for the body to digest, leaving you feeling fuller for longer, so you are less likely to overeat.

Salads aren't just for summer. By using seasonal ingredients, such as asparagus in late spring, lettuce in summer, squashes in fall, and root vegetables, kale, grains, and dried beans in winter, you can enjoy a healthy diet all year round.

Salads don't have to be cold either; they can include, for example, warm grains, roasted vegetables, strips of seared steak, or stir-fried shrimp. In colder months, you can add heat to dressings with spices, grated fresh ginger, and garlic.

Preparing salad greens

Greens are delicate and can bruise easily. They need washing; even bags of prewashed greens benefit from a rinse because they tend to have been washed with chlorinelike chemicals when packaged. Separate the leaves, then put them in a sink of cold water, turn them to loosen, and remove any dirt, then drain in a colander. Pat dry with a clean dish towel or dry in a salad spinner. Any unused greens can be packed into a plastic box or bag, sealed, and stored in the vegetable compartment in the bottom of the refrigerator. Add dressings at the last minute so the greens don't wilt.

Salad greens who's who

A huge range of salad greens is sold in the stores. But why not grow your own? Arugula, baby Swiss chard, and mizuna are all easy to grow in a small flower bed, flowerpot, or windowsill box, and the first leaves can be harvested within six weeks of planting.

Arugula — Small peppery leaves with jagged edges and a hot flavor.

Bibb lettuce and Boston lettuce — Both are a small butterhead-type lettuce, with loose leaves and plenty of flavor; Bibb is smaller than Boston lettuce, and also more expensive.

Butterhead or basic round lettuce — Soft, round lettuce with a pale green heart. It doesn't keep well, so use on the day of purchase.

Curly endive — Sometimes called frisée, curly endive is a member of the chicory family. The spreading, frondlike leaves taste a little bitter. It can be made into a salad on its own or mixed with other greens.

Dandelion — Not readily available at supermarkets, but young dark leaves can be picked from the backyard if you don't use chemicals, although they must be washed well before being eaten. They are at their best in spring. Older leaves need cooking.

Endive — Pale, tight head of spear-shape leaves with pale green or red tips and a crisp, bitter flavor.

Iceberg — A large, crisp, crunchy, densely packed lettuce that keeps well in the refrigerator.

Mâche — Or corn salad, form tiny clumps of soft, mild buttery leaves that are shaped like lambs' tongues, which is another name. Popular in France and Italy.

Mizuna — Similar in looks to dandelion leaves, with a delicate peppery flavor.

Mustard leaf — Baby leaves with an elongated shape and purple edges.

Pea shoots — With their delicate, tender tendrils, they make a pretty garnish.

Radicchio — A deep-red, tightly packed head of leaves that is part of the chicory family. Mix it with other ingredients because its flavor is strong.

Red-tinged greens — Examples include slightly bitter escarole and mild, tender, and frilly lollo rosso and oakleaf. The leaves range in color from red to deep russet-brown (and also green), with leaves becoming greener the nearer the heart you go.

Romaine lettuce — Long, thin lettuces with dark green outer leaves that change to pale green at the heart. They are used to make the classic Caesar salad.

Spinach — The crisp, mildly bitter leaves add contrast when mixed with milder-tasting ones.

Swiss chard leaves — Red-veined green leaves with red stems. Ruby Swiss chard has deep red leaves and stems. Also try small newly shooting leaves of Swiss chard or beet.

Watercress — One of the cresses, which include upland cress, curly cress, and land cress; it has a tart, peppery flavor and rounded petal-like leaves.

Beyond greens

Energy-boosting fruit and vegetables — These can offer complex carbohydrates for slow-release energy and soluble and insoluble dietary fiber, which aids sustained absorption of sugar into the blood stream.

Protein plus — Turn a simple salad into a protein-boosting main meal with the addition of a little broiled steak, chicken, turkey, salmon, sea bass, or other fish, or add a few stir-fried shrimp. Alternatively, add tofu, a sprinkling of crumbled feta cheese, diced Brie, or a few Parmesan shavings. In the West, we eat more protein than our bodies need, but if you cut these ingredients into strips, shreds, or dice, a little goes a long way, and you can serve smaller portions without anyone really noticing. Nutritionists recommend eating just a 4-ounce portion of red meat per serving.

Vitamin boosters — For boosting beta-carotene, choose orange-flesh melons, pumpkins, carrots, papayas, mangoes, dark green leafy vegetables, red bell peppers, and tomatoes. Good sources of vitamin C include bell peppers, green leafy vegetables, kale, broccoli, citrus fruits, berries, mangoes, and papayas.

Mineral-boosting nuts and seeds — These provide vitamin E, iron, zinc, magnesium, protein, and fiber. Some seeds, such as flaxseeds (also called linseeds), provide omega-3 fatty acids. Nuts (except for coconut) are high in monounsaturated fats, while seeds are high in polyunsaturated fats; both are good fats. Although this increases their calories, a small sprinkle goes a long way.

Healthy whole grains — Choose from wheatberries, buckwheat, bulgur wheat, whole-wheat couscous, quinoa, pearl barley, oat groats, and lentils. All are rich in protein, complex carbs, and a wide range of vitamins and minerals. They are also high in soluble fiber to help reduce cholesterol and insoluble fiber for healthy digestion. Quinoa is the only grain that contains all the essential amino acids. Unlike meat proteins, most grains need to be eaten with a second protein source.

How to make vinaigrette

The traditional blend for this classic French dressing is a ratio of three parts oil to one part vinegar, with a little salt and pepper plus a flavoring of your choice. These proportions can be tweaked depending on the acidity of the vinegar or strength or flavor of the oil.

The key to a good vinaigrette is to whisk the vinegar with an emulsifier, such as 1 teaspoon of Dijon mustard, a finely chopped shallot, or 1 teaspoon of honey. Gradually whisk in the oil, drop by drop, until the texture is smooth and thick and the vinegar and oil have emulsified together to make a creamy dressing. The more you whisk, the thicker the dressing will be.

If the dressing is too thin or has separated, start again in a clean, small bowl with an extra teaspoon of mustard or a tablespoon of heavy cream or plain yogurt, then slowly whisk in the dressing until smooth once more.

Check the seasoning and the balance of the oil and vinegar once the dressing is made, and adjust if needed. Taste again once the salad is dressed. There are so few ingredients in a good vinaigrette that getting the balance right is critical.

To flavor your dressing, try whisking in a little finely chopped fresh tarragon, chives, parsley, or garlic. For an Asian twist, add a dash of soy sauce and a little finely grated fresh ginger. For something with heat, add a seeded and finely chopped red chile, a few drops of Tabasco sauce and Worcestershire sauce, or even a little Cognac. Other good flavorings include toasted and coarsely crushed coriander, cumin, or fennel seeds, a little tomato paste, or a sprinkling of finely chopped aromatic herbs, such as fresh mint or cilantro leaves.

Choosing an oil

Olive oil is often the first choice for salad dressings. Choose from dark green extra virgin, virgin, or light olive oil (a golden oil made from the last pressing). They vary greatly in flavor, depending on which country or region they come from, ranging from peppery to salty to fruity to creamy to mild. A good source of vitamin E and high in flavonoids and monounsaturated fatty acids, unheated olive oils aren't thought to raise blood cholesterol levels and may help lower them.

Nut oils, such as walnut or hazelnut oil, add a strong flavor to dressings. However, they also tend to be expensive. They are best mixed half-and-half with a milder oil. Sesame oil, which is made from roasted and crushed sesame seeds, also has a strong flavor, which is smoky, and it is combined mainly with Asian ingredients.

Look for flaxseed and hemp seed oils. Like olive oil, they are produced with minimal heat. Some are made by cold-pressing refining processes, so they retain more phytochemicals and essential fatty acids. They tend to be produced without herbicides, pesticides, bleaches, or deodorizing.

Hemp oil is naturally rich in omega-3 fatty acids; a single tablespoon contains almost 100 percent of an adult's daily recommended intake. It is also thought to contribute to your hair, skin, immune system, and joint health, and it is believed to have some anti-inflammatory properties.

Rice bran oil, which has a light flavor, also makes a healthy option. It is rich in vitamin E and can be used in cooking. Safflower and sunflower oils are rich in omega-6 fatty acids, but these, along with vegetable oil blends and grapeseed oil, tend to be more processed than other oils.

Keep nut and seed oils in a cool dark place, preferably in the refrigerator, once opened. It's best to buy them in small quantities.

Choosing a vinegar

Choose from red or white wine vinegar, or try cider, sherry, or balsamic. Sherry vinegar has a rich, deep flavor but is lighter than balsamic. True balsamic vinegar is an artisan product from Modena in Italy and is made from pressed grape juice that has been fermented in wooden barrels for years to give it a sweet, tangy, mellow taste. It is so full of flavor that you can use it as a salad dressing on its own.

Easy vinaigrette

For a simple vinaigrette, put a tablespoon of white or red wine vinegar and 3 tablespoons of olive oil in a screw-top jar. Add a teaspoon each of Dijon mustard and honey and season with salt and pepper. Screw on the lid, then shake well. The more you shake the dressing, the more emulsified it will be. It won't be as thick as if you trickle in the oil, but it will be delicious.

All dressed up

Vinaigrette — This is the classic oil-and-vinegar salad dressing. You can flavor it with Dijon or whole-grain mustard, a finely chopped shallot, or finely chopped fresh herbs, and sweeten it with a little honey. Whisk the ingredients together, adding the oil gradually to create a smooth emulsion.

Low-fat and healthy dressings — Mayonnaise and sour cream or blue cheese dressings are loaded with calories. To reduce their fat, mix them half-and-half with plain yogurt. For a more low-calorie dressing, mix virtually fat-free plain yogurt with chopped fresh herbs, finely chopped garlic, and crushed peppercorns or ground spices, or a mix of all three, and add a small sprinkling of sweetener. For a zingy, light, vitamin C-boosting dressing, try freshly squeezed lemon, lime, or orange juice seasoned with salt and pepper. A few flaxseeds make a healthy addition to a dressing.

Dairy-free dressings — Try a mixture of orange or lemon juice, a little Dijon mustard, and a splash of aged balsamic vinegar. Also try lime juice mixed with finely grated fresh ginger and soy sauce. There is a wide choice of oils, such as sunflower, olive, seed, and nut oils, and vinegars, such as sherry, red, or white wine.

Classic vinaigrette

Dairy-free dressings

Healthy dressings

Low-fat dressings

Refresh

Classic melon, prosciutto & pecorino salad

Per serving: 328 cals   21.3g fat   5.2g sat fat   17.2g protein   22.7g carbs   2.2g fiber

You can enjoy a lovely big bowl of this fresh-tasting salad without feeling guilty, because the melon is deliciously low in calories! With the salty hit from the ham and pecorino and the refreshing, water-packed melon, it's a perfect lunch for a hot day.

Serves 4

* ⅛ watermelon, peeled, seeded, and thinly sliced
* ½ honeydew melon, peeled, seeded, and thinly sliced
* ½ cantaloupe, peeled, seeded, and thinly sliced
* 5 ounces sliced prosciutto
* 1 ounce pecorino cheese shavings
* ⅔ cup fresh basil

Dressing

* ¼ cup light olive oil
* ¼ cup aged sherry vinegar
* salt and pepper, to taste

How to make it

Arrange the watermelon, honeydew melon, and cantaloupe slices on a large serving plate. Tear any large prosciutto slices in half, then fold all the slices over and around the melon.

To make the dressing, put the olive oil and sherry vinegar in a screw-top jar, season well with salt and pepper, screw on the lid, and shake well. Drizzle the dressing over the melon and prosciutto.

Sprinkle with the pecorino and basil. Serve immediately.

Melon detox

Melons are low in calories, containing just 19–31 calories per 3½ ounces flesh (about ⅔ cup diced), depending on type. The more orange the melon's flesh, the more beneficial beta-carotene it contains. Beta-carotene works with vitamins C and E and minerals to help protect our cells from the harmful effects of oxidation caused by pollution, pesticide residues, smoking, and stress.

Refreshing seared beef salad

Per serving: 352 cals 20g fat 3.5g sat fat 31.6g protein 15g carbs 2.9g fiber

A Thai-inspired salad with wafer-thin sliced seared steak served over sliced peppery radishes, nutrient-boosting kale, cool mint, and cilantro, all drizzled with a zesty lime dressing.

Serves 4

* ½ iceberg lettuce, leaves separated and torn into bite-size pieces
* 1¾ cups thinly sliced radishes
* 4 shallots, thinly sliced
* 1¼ cups shredded kale
* 2 tablespoons dried goji berries
* ½ cup coarsely chopped fresh mint
* ½ cup coarsely chopped fresh cilantro
* 2 (8-ounce) tenderloin steaks, visible fat removed
* ¼ cup sunflower oil
* juice of 1 lime
* 1 tablespoon soy sauce
* salt and pepper, to taste

Crunch time

Put the lettuce, radishes, and shallots in a serving bowl. Sprinkle with the kale, goji berries, mint, and cilantro, then toss gently together.

Preheat a heavy, ridged grill pan over high heat. Brush the steaks with 1 tablespoon of oil, then sprinkle with a little salt and pepper. Cook in the hot pan for 2 minutes on each side for medium—rare, 3 minutes on each side for medium, or 4 minutes on each side for well done. Transfer the steaks to a plate and leave to rest for a few minutes.

Meanwhile, to make the dressing, put the lime juice, soy sauce, and remaining 3 tablespoons of oil in a screw-top jar, screw on the lid, and shake well. Drizzle the dressing over the salad, then toss together.

Divide the salad among four bowls. Thinly slice the steak and arrange it over the top, then serve immediately.

Mint for your stomach

Mint leaves freshen the palate and are rich in chlorophyll, antioxidants, and the essential oils menthol, menthone, and menthol acetate. Mint is thought to help relieve symptoms of irritable bowel syndrome by relieving bloating and abdominal discomfort.

Light tamarind turkey salad

Per serving: 302 cals 15.2g fat 1.8g sat fat 29.2g protein 14g carbs 1.8g fiber

Tamarind gives this salad a tart, sour flavor that works wonderfully with the sweet orange juice and maple syrup. The tangy dressing doubles up as a sticky glaze for the stir-fried turkey — wonderful!

Serves 4

* ¼ cup sunflower oil
* 1 pound raw turkey breast slices, cut into small dice
* ½ iceberg lettuce, leaves separated and torn into bite-size pieces
* ½ head of endive, leaves separated
* 1¼ cups shredded kale
* 1⅓ cups diced cucumber
* ½ small red onion, sliced
* orange zest strips, to garnish

Dressing

* 2 teaspoons tamarind paste, any seeds removed
* finely grated zest and juice of 1 orange
* ¾-inch piece of fresh ginger, peeled and finely grated
* 2 garlic cloves, finely chopped
* 4 teaspoons maple syrup
* salt and pepper, to taste

Mix it up

To make the dressing, put the tamarind paste, orange zest and juice, ginger, garlic, and maple syrup in a small bowl, season with salt and pepper, and mix together well.

To make the salad, heat 2 tablespoons of the oil in a large skillet over medium—high heat. Add the turkey and stir-fry for 5 minutes, or until golden and cooked through; cut into the middle of a piece to check that the meat is no longer pink and that the juices are clear and piping hot. Add half the dressing and cook for another 2—3 minutes, or until the turkey is glazed and shiny. Transfer the turkey to a plate and set aside.

Put the lettuce, endive, and kale in a salad bowl, and sprinkle with the cucumber and onion.

Mix the remaining 2 tablespoons of oil into the remaining dressing. Drizzle the dressing over the salad, then toss gently together. Divide the salad between four bowls and sprinkle the warm, glazed turkey on top. Garnish with the orange zest and serve.

Good for your heart!

Eating loads of fruit and vegetables can help protect you from heart disease and reduce your risk of stroke by up to 30 percent.

Fruity chicken salad

Per serving: 229 cals 8.4g fat 1g sat fat 21.6g protein 18.6g carbs 4g fiber

This superhealthy take on coleslaw is bursting with zingy citrus fruit, crunchy green cabbage, and thin shreds of kale, all tossed in a light lime vinaigrette instead of the classic mayonnaise dressing.

Serves 4

* 2 tablespoons sunflower oil
* 8 ounces boneless, skinless chicken breasts, sliced
* ¼ teaspoon crushed red pepper flakes
* 1 pink grapefruit, peeled with a knife and cut into segments, membrane reserved
* 1 orange, peeled with a knife and cut into segments, membrane reserved
* 1 small mango, halved, pitted, peeled, and diced
* 2⅓ cups thinly shredded green cabbage
* ¾ cup thinly shredded kale
* salt and pepper, to taste

Dressing

* juice of 1 lime
* 1 teaspoon Dijon mustard
* ¾-inch piece of fresh ginger, peeled and finely grated

Make it now!

Heat 1 tablespoon of the oil in a skillet over medium—high heat. Add the chicken, sprinkle with the red pepper flakes, and season with a little salt and pepper. Cook for 8—10 minutes, turning once or twice, or until golden and cooked through; cut into the middle of a piece to check that the meat is no longer pink and that the juices are clear and piping hot. Transfer the chicken to a plate.

Put the grapefruit and orange segments in a salad bowl, then add the mango, cabbage, and kale and toss.

To make the dressing, squeeze the juice from the citrus membranes into a screw-top jar. Add the lime juice, mustard, ginger, and remaining 1 tablespoon of oil, then season with salt and pepper. Screw on the lid and shake well. Drizzle the dressing over the salad, then toss gently together.

Divide the salad among four bowls, cut the fried chicken into shreds, sprinkle it over the top, then serve.

Light tamarind
turkey salad

page 18

Fruity chicken
salad

page 19

Broiled sea bass & citrus salad

Bursting with vitamins and minerals, this light, zesty salad with lime-marinated broiled sea bass will leave you feeling fresh and ready to go!

Serves 4

* 3 cups baby spinach
* 1½ cups mâche
* 1½ cups ruby Swiss chard leaves
* 2 ruby grapefruits, peeled with a knife and cut into segments, membrane reserved
* 1 orange, peeled with a knife and cut into segments, membrane reserved
* 4 sea bass fillets
* finely grated zest and juice of 1 lime
* 3 tablespoons olive oil
* 1 teaspoon honey
* salt and pepper, to taste
* 2 tablespoons finely chopped fresh cilantro, to garnish

Time to get started

Put the spinach, mâche, and Swiss chard leaves in a salad bowl, then add the grapefruit and orange segments. Squeeze the juice from the citrus membranes into a screw-top jar and reserve.

Preheat the broiler to hot and line the broiler pan with aluminum foil. Arrange the sea bass, flesh side up, on the foil, sprinkle with the lime zest and juice, and season with salt and pepper. Turn the fish over, season with salt and pepper, and drizzle with 1 tablespoon of olive oil. Broil for 6–8 minutes, turning once, or until the skin is browned and the fish is opaque and flakes when pressed.

To make the dressing, add the remaining olive oil and the honey to the fruit juice in the jar, season with salt and pepper, screw on the lid, and shake well. Drizzle the dressing over the salad and toss gently together, then divide among four plates.

Break each fish fillet into bite-size pieces, then arrange them on top of the salads. Sprinkle with the cilantro, spoon over any juices from the broiler pan, then serve immediately.

Per serving: 260 cals 6.7g fat 1.2g sat fat 30g protein 20.7g carbs 3.5g fiber

Go citrus crazy!

The colorful citrus family includes oranges, kumquats, lemons, limes, grapefruits, tangerines, pomelos, and other hybrid citrus fruits, and contains some of the richest fruit sources of vitamin C. One medium-to-large orange provides twice the Recommended National Intake (RNI) of this vitamin. Vital to aid the absorption of iron, which is especially important if you eat little meat, vitamin C also helps us fight infection and boosts the immune system. It is thought it may help with nasal inflammation, so reducing the symptoms of a cold, catarrh, hay fever, and even rheumatism. A high intake of vitamin C may also lower the risk of coronary heart disease by up to 40 percent and slow down the effects of skin aging. Pink grapefruit and blood oranges also contain good amounts of beta-carotene, while lemons contain limonene, a phytochemical that is thought to help protect against cancer.

Seafood supersalad

Per serving: 272 cals   15.7g fat   2.3g sat fat   22g protein   10.2g carbs   0.5g fiber

Seafood is as refreshing as sea air—but you don't have to travel to the coast
to enjoy this deliciously fresh-tasting salad!

Serves 4

* 8 ounces fresh mussels, scrubbed and debearded
* 12 ounces fresh scallops, shucked and cleaned
* 8 ounces cleaned and prepared squid, cut into rings and tentacles
* 1 red onion, thinly sliced
* 1 lemon, cut into 4 wedges, to serve

Dressing

* ¼ cup extra virgin olive oil
* 2 tablespoons white wine vinegar
* 1 tablespoon lemon juice
* 1 garlic clove, finely chopped
* 1 tablespoon finely chopped fresh flat-leaf parsley, plus 1 tablespoon, to garnish
* salt and pepper, to taste

Toss your salad

Discard any mussels with broken shells or that refuse to close when tapped. Put the remaining mussels in a colander and rinse well under cold running water. Transfer them to a large saucepan, add a little water, and cook, covered, over high heat, shaking occasionally, for 3—4 minutes, or until they have opened. Discard any that remain closed. Strain the mussels, reserving the cooking liquid, then refresh them under cold running water, drain, and set aside.

Return the reserved cooking liquid to the pan and bring to a boil. Add the scallops and squid and cook for 3 minutes. Remove from the heat and drain. Refresh them under cold running water, drain again, and set aside.

Remove the cooked mussels from their shells and put them in a bowl. Add the scallops and squid, then let cool. Cover with plastic wrap and chill in the refrigerator for 45 minutes. Divide the seafood among four bowls, add the onion, and toss gently together.

To make the dressing, put the oil, vinegar, lemon juice, garlic, and parsley in a screw-top jar, season with salt and pepper, screw on the lid, and shake well. Drizzle the dressing over the salads and garnish with the parsley. Serve, with the lemon wedges for squeezing over.

Super seafood

Seafood is generally rich in protein, vitamins, and minerals, yet low in calories. Shellfish is a good source of the trace minerals selenium and zinc, which work with vitamin E for normal body growth and fertility.

Chile squid salad

Per serving: 506 cals 37.7g fat 5.5g sat fat 29.2g protein 13g carbs 1.2g fiber

A tangy lime-dressed mixture of seared squid, red chile, and scallions, served with cool, crisp, iron-rich leaves, guaranteed to wake up and refresh those taste-buds.

Serves 4

* 1½ pounds cleaned and prepared squid, cut into tubes and tentacles
* 3 tablespoons olive oil
* 1 red chile, seeded and thinly sliced
* 2 scallions, finely chopped
* a squeeze of lemon juice, plus lemon wedges, to serve
* 3 cups watercress
* 2½ cups baby spinach
* salt and pepper, to taste

Dressing

* ½ cup olive oil
* juice of 1 lime
* 1 teaspoon honey
* 2 shallots, thinly sliced
* 1 tomato, peeled, seeded, and finely chopped
* 1 garlic clove, crushed

Make it now!

To make the dressing, put all the ingredients in a small bowl, season with salt and pepper, mix together well, cover, and refrigerate until required.

Cut the squid tubes into 2-inch pieces, then score diamond patterns lightly across the flesh, using the tip of a sharp knife. Heat the oil in a large skillet over high heat. Add the squid pieces and tentacles and stir-fry for 1 minute. Add the chile and scallions and stir-fry for an additional minute. Season well with salt and pepper and add a good squeeze of lemon juice.

Put the watercress and spinach in a salad bowl, then add the cooked squid. Drizzle enough dressing to coat lightly over the salad and toss gently together. Serve immediately, with the lemon wedges for squeezing over.

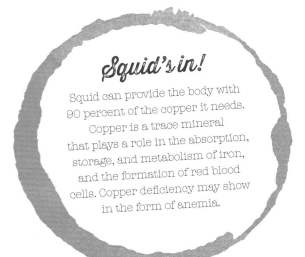

Squid's in!

Squid can provide the body with 90 percent of the copper it needs. Copper is a trace mineral that plays a role in the absorption, storage, and metabolism of iron, and the formation of red blood cells. Copper deficiency may show in the form of anemia.

Cool watermelon, goat cheese & arugula salad

Per serving: 207 cals 11g fat 7.1g sat fat 11g protein 19.4g carbs 1.8g fiber

The delicate creaminess of the goat cheese in this salad complements the citrus- and chile-dressed watermelon to make a deliciously quick and rehydrating summer salad that will have you coming back for more.

Serves 4

* 5¼ cups large watermelon cubes
* grated zest and juice of 2 large limes, plus lime wedges, to serve
* ½–1 red chile, seeded and finely chopped
* 1¼ cups coarsely chopped fresh cilantro
* 3 cups arugula
* 4 ounces firm goat cheese, cut into cubes
* salt and pepper, to taste

Mix it up

Put the watermelon in a large salad bowl. Sprinkle with the lime zest and juice and the chile, then season with a little salt and pepper and toss gently together.

Sprinkle with the cilantro, arugula, and goat cheese and toss gently together. Serve with lime wedges.

Thirst-quenching watermelon

It is recommended that we drink six to eight glasses of water a day, but don't forget that our foods can contribute to our water intake, too. Watermelon is about 80 percent water, plus ripe watermelons contain a powerful antioxidant, glutathione, which is known to help boost the immune system and fight infection.

Roasted pepper pep-up salad

Per serving: 321 cals 27.5g fat 5.7g sat fat 7.6g protein 12.3g carbs 2.8g fiber

Capture the taste of the Mediterranean with this roasted antioxidant-rich bell pepper salad.

Serves 4

* 2 red bell peppers, halved and seeded
* 2 yellow bell peppers, halved and seeded
* 1 red onion, coarsely chopped
* 2 garlic cloves, finely chopped
* ⅓ cup olive oil
* 4 ounces mini mozzarella cheese pearls, drained
* 2 tablespoons coarsely torn fresh basil
* 2 tablespoons balsamic vinegar
* salt and pepper, to taste

Time to get started

Preheat the oven to 375°F. Put the bell peppers, cut side up, in a shallow roasting pan. Sprinkle with the onion and garlic, season well with salt and pepper, and drizzle with 3 tablespoons of the olive oil. Roast for 40 minutes, or until the peppers are tender. Let cool.

Arrange the cold bell peppers in a serving dish, and pour any juices left in the roasting pan over them. Sprinkle with the mozzarella and basil.

To make the dressing, whisk together the remaining olive oil and the balsamic vinegar, then drizzle the dressing over the bell peppers. Cover and let marinate in the refrigerator for at least 2 hours before serving.

Power bell peppers

All bell peppers are rich in vitamins A, C, and K, but red bell peppers are simply bursting with them. The antioxidant vitamins A and C help to prevent cell damage, cancer, and diseases related to aging, and they support immune function. They also reduce inflammation, such as that found in arthritis and asthma.

Oh-so-good-for-you Greek feta salad

Per serving: 208 cals 17.4g fat 5.8g sat fat 5.8g protein 8.8g carbs 1.8g fiber

A Mediterranean diet, rich in olive oil, sun-kissed vegetables, and lemons, has long been recognized as healthy, and this simple, tasty salad is no exception. However, it will only taste as good as the tomatoes you choose.

Serves 4

* 4 blanched grape leaves, drained
* 3 tomatoes, thinly sliced
* ½ cucumber, peeled and thinly sliced
* 1 small red onion, thinly sliced
* 4 ounces feta cheese (drained weight), cut into cubes
* 32 black ripe olives, stoned

Dressing

* 3 tablespoons extra virgin olive oil
* 1 tablespoon lemon juice
* ½ teaspoon dried oregano
* salt and pepper, to taste

How to make it

Arrange the grape leaves on four plates. Top with the tomatoes, cucumber, and onion, then the feta and olives.

To make the dressing, put the oil, lemon juice, and dried oregano in a screw-top jar, screw on the lid, and shake well. Drizzle the dressing over the salad, season with salt and pepper, then serve immediately.

Feta is fab

Feta cheese is made with sheep or goat milk. It contains calcium, which helps keep your bones strong and can help to prevent osteoporosis. It also contains vitamin B$_{12}$, which helps with brain function. So say yes to feta!

Spiced beet & cucumber tzatziki

Per serving: 50 cals   0.8g fat   0.5g sat fat   4.8g protein   6.6g carbs   1.5g fiber

These mini bites make a perfect appetizer, and they are delicious served as part of a mixed selection of nibbles to go with drinks.

Serves 4

* ¾ cup diced, drained cooked beet in natural juices
* ½ cucumber, diced
* 10 radishes, diced
* 1 scallion, finely chopped
* 12 Bibb or Boston lettuce leaves

Dressing

* ⅔ cup 2 percent fat Greek-style plain yogurt
* ¼ teaspoon ground cumin
* ½ teaspoon honey
* 2 tablespoons finely chopped fresh mint
* salt and pepper, to taste

Toss your salad

To make the dressing, put the yogurt, cumin, and honey in a bowl, then stir in the mint and season with salt and pepper.

Add the beet, cucumber, radishes, and scallion, then toss gently together.

Arrange the lettuce leaves on a plate. Spoon a little of the salad into each leaf. Serve immediately.

Love lettuce

The outer leaves of a lettuce contain the most beta-carotene and vitamin C, with small amounts of folate and iron. Lettuce is thought by herbalists to calm the nerves and aid sleep.

Bitter greens with palate-cleansing citrus dressing

Per serving: 103 cals 7g fat 1.2g sat fat 1.5g protein 9.6g carbs 1.8g fiber

Capture the essence of summer with this baby leaf salad tossed with bitter curly endive lettuce in a zesty orange and lemon dressing with a hint of soy.

Serves 4

* ¼ curly endive, torn into bite-size pieces
* 2 cups baby spinach
* 2½ cups mixed baby greens
* ¾ cup blueberries
* a few edible viola and nasturtium flowers (optional), to garnish

Dressing

* finely grated zest and juice of ½ small orange, plus extra finely grated zest, to garnish
* finely grated zest and juice of ½ unwaxed lemon, plus extra finely grated zest, to garnish
* 1 tablespoon light soy sauce
* 2 tablespoons rice bran oil
* 1 teaspoon honey
* pepper, to taste

Flower power

Put the curly endive, spinach, and baby greens in a large salad bowl. Sprinkle with the blueberries.

To make the dressing, put the orange and lemon zest and juice, soy sauce, oil, and honey in a screw-top jar, season with pepper, screw on the lid, and shake well. Drizzle the dressing over the salad, then toss gently together. Serve on four plates, garnished with the flowers, if using, and orange and lemon zest.

Beautiful blueberries

With their high antioxidant levels, blueberries not only help to protect us against cancer, but also to stabilize brain function and protect neural tissue from oxidative stress (which may improve memory and learning and reduce symptoms of depression).

Big cranberry bean, tomato & onion salad with eggs

Per serving: 503 cals   26.6g fat   2g sat fat   23g protein   44.5g carbs   17g fiber

The lemon dressing gives this salad a refreshing, zesty flavor and complements the earthy beans perfectly.

Serves 4

* 1¼ cups dried cranberry beans, soaked overnight or for at least 8 hours
* 2 large garlic cloves, crushed
* juice of 2 lemons
* ⅓ cup extra virgin olive oil
* 1 teaspoon salt
* 1 small onion, finely chopped
* 2 tomatoes, seeded and finely chopped
* ⅔ cup finely chopped fresh flat-leaf parsley
* 1 teaspoon cumin seeds, crushed
* pepper, to taste

Garnish

* 4 eggs
* 1 lemon, cut into 4 wedges
* pinch of sumac or crushed red pepper flakes

Time to get started

Drain and rinse the beans, put them in a large saucepan, cover with fresh cold water, and bring to a boil. Boil rapidly for at least 10 minutes, then remove from the heat, drain, and rinse again. Add fresh cold water, bring to a boil, then simmer for 1½–2 hours, or until tender, adding more boiling water, if needed. Drain and transfer to a shallow serving dish.

For the garnish, put the eggs in a saucepan and pour in enough cold water to cover them by ½ inch. Bring to a boil, then reduce to a simmer and cook for 8 minutes. Drain immediately, cool quickly under cold running water, then peel and cut into quarters.

Lightly crush some of the warm beans with the back of a spoon. Add the garlic, lemon juice, olive oil, and salt while the beans are warm and mix together. Add the onion, tomatoes, parsley, and cumin, and season with pepper, then toss gently together. Arrange the hard-boiled eggs and lemon wedges on top, sprinkle with the sumac, and serve.

Gingered carrot & pomegranate salad

Per serving: 179 cals   10.7g fat   1.5g sat fat   2g protein   20g carbs   4.2g fiber

Turn a humble carrot into an exotic, fresh-tasting salad with a little Middle Eastern magic with the help of jewel-like pomegranate.

Serves 4

* 6 carrots, finely grated
* 2-inch piece of fresh ginger, peeled and finely grated
* 1 small pomegranate, quartered
* 1½ cups ready-to-eat alfalfa sprouts, radish sprouts, or other sprouts

Dressing

* 3 tablespoons light olive oil
* 3 teaspoons red wine vinegar
* 3 teaspoons pomegranate molasses
* salt and pepper, to taste

Mix it up

Put the carrots and ginger in a salad bowl. Flex the pomegranate pieces to pop out the seeds, prying any stubborn ones out with the tip of a small knife, and add to the bowl.

To make the dressing, put the oil, vinegar, and pomegranate molasses in a screw-top jar, season with salt and pepper, screw on the lid, and shake well. Drizzle the dressing over the salad and toss gently together. Cover and let marinate in the refrigerator for 30 minutes.

Sprinkle the sprouts over the salad and serve.

Pomegranate jewels

The pomegranate's glistening rubylike seeds might be tiny, but they pack a punch. They are rich in flavonoids and polyphenols, antioxidants thought to help protect against heart disease and cancer.

Zesty avocado, pineapple & pink grapefruit salad

Per serving: 150 cals   6g fat   0.8g sat fat   2g protein   26g carbs   5.5g fiber

Wake up those taste-buds with this superzingy fresh fruity salad. Prettily served in an iceberg lettuce cup, it makes a perfect appetizer or side dish.

Serves 4

* 2 pink grapefruits, peeled with a knife and cut into segments, membrane reserved
* ½ pineapple, sliced, peeled, cored, and diced
* 1 large avocado, halved, pitted, peeled, and diced
* finely grated zest and juice of 1 lime
* 2 tablespoons finely chopped fresh mint
* 4 outer iceberg lettuce leaves

How to make it

Halve each grapefruit segment, then put them in a salad bowl. Squeeze the juice from the membrane over the segments. Add the pineapple and avocado, sprinkle with the lime zest and juice and mint, then toss gently together.

Arrange a lettuce leaf on each of four small plates. Spoon some salad into the center of each lettuce leaf and serve immediately.

Pineapple pick-me-up

Vitamin C-rich pineapple and grapefruit help boost the body's immune system and the production of collagen needed for healthy skin, bones, cartilage, teeth, and gums. Vitamin C may even also be a key protective element against cardiovascular disease, cancer, and asthma.

Baby leaf remedy salad with raspberry dressing

Per serving: 150 cals   11.2g fat   1.4g sat fat   2.4g protein   12g carbs   4.2g fiber

A fresh raspberry dressing is gently tossed with stomach-soothing summer salad greens and antioxidant-rich goji berries.

Serves 4

* 4½ cups bistro salad (a mixture of baby red Swiss chard varieties and mâche)
* 1 cup arugula
* ⅓ cup pea shoots
* 1½ cups raspberries
* 3 tablespoons dried goji berries

Dressing

* 1 teaspoon honey
* 1 tablespoon red wine vinegar
* 3 tablespoons light olive oil
* salt and pepper, to taste

Pretty in pink

Put the bistro salad, arugula, and pea shoots in a salad bowl, then toss gently together.

To make the dressing, put ½ cup of the raspberries, the honey, vinegar, and oil in a blender, season with salt and pepper, then process until smooth.

Serve the salad greens on small plates, sprinkled with the remaining raspberries and the goji berries, along with the dressing for drizzling over the salad.

Raspberry boost

Raspberries are rich in vitamin C. Herbalists also suggest using raspberry vinegar to help coughs.

Exotic coconut cooler

Per serving: 390 cals 25.9g fat 22.3g sat fat 5.2g protein 41g carbs 10.7g fiber

Awaken those taste-buds and transport them to Jamaica with this tropical salad, which combines juicy, lightly perfumed mango, sweet, refreshing pineapple, and crunchy, fresh coconut speckled with tiny ruby goji berries.

Serves 4

* 1 small coconut
* finely grated zest and juice of 1 lime
* 1 small pineapple, sliced, peeled, cored, and diced
* 1 large mango, halved, pitted, peeled, and diced
* ½ cucumber, peeled, halved lengthwise, seeded, and thickly sliced
* 3 tablespoons dried goji berries
* 1 cup finely chopped fresh cilantro

Tropical dreams

Pierce one of the three eyes in the bottom of the coconut using a barbecue skewer or a sharp knife, then drain out the liquid, strain it through a strainer, and reserve. Break the rest of the coconut into pieces.

To make the dressing, mix the coconut milk and lime zest and juice together in a salad bowl. Pry the flesh away from the hard coconut shell, using a small pointed knife, then pare it into thin shavings, using a swivel-blade vegetable peeler, to make about 1 cup.

Add the coconut shavings to the dressing, then add the pineapple, mango, cucumber, goji berries, and cilantro and toss gently together. Spoon into four bowls and serve immediately.

The five-a-day way!

At least 50 percent of your calories should come from plant-base foods, so aim to eat a minimum of five portions of vegetables and fruit every day.

Energy

Sweet & sour crispy pork with gingered noodle salad

Per serving: 461 cals 10.5g fat 1.7g sat fat 40g protein 48g carbs 4.4g fiber

Made up of a good mix of complex carbs and fiber, this light, fresh-tasting salad will provide a slow-release energy boost. It can be prepared the night before and stored in the refrigerator, then taken to work in a plastic container for a healthy office lunch.

Serves 4

* 1¼ pounds lean pork cutlets
* 8 ounces dried whole-wheat Chinese noodles
* 2 cups shredded Chinese greens
* 2 carrots, cut into thin matchsticks
* 2 cups thinly sliced snow peas
* 2 scallions, finely chopped
* ¾-inch piece of fresh ginger, peeled and finely grated

Dressing

* finely grated zest and juice of ½ orange
* 2 tablespoons sunflower oil
* 2 tablespoons soy sauce
* 1 tablespoon honey
* 1 tablespoon rice vinegar
* 1 teaspoon star anise pieces, ground
* 2 garlic cloves, finely chopped

Oodles of noodles

Preheat the broiler to high and line the broiler pan with aluminum foil. To make the dressing, put the orange zest and juice, oil, soy sauce, honey, vinegar, star anise, and garlic in a screw-top jar, screw on the lid, and shake well.

Arrange the pork on the broiler pan in a single layer and spoon 3 tablespoons of the dressing over the meat. Broil for 12–15 minutes, turning the pork and spooning the juices over once or twice, until browned and cooked through.

Meanwhile, cook the noodles according to the package directions. Drain into a colander, rinse with cold water, then drain again. Put them in a salad bowl, pour over the remaining dressing, and let cool.

Add the Chinese greens, carrots, snow peas, scallions, and ginger to the salad bowl and toss gently together. Thinly slice the pork and arrange it over the salad, then serve.

Foods for energy

We need energy to breathe, move, exercise, grow, and pump blood around our bodies. It comes mainly from carbohydrates, but also from fat and protein. Carbs should provide at least 50 percent, fat no more than 35 percent, and protein a maximum of 15 percent of our daily diet.

Spinach & pancetta power salad

Per serving: 413 cals   36.5g fat   8.9g sat fat   16.2g protein   6.4g carbs   3.7g fiber

The sweet, sticky dressing perfectly enhances the smoky pancetta and slightly bitter spinach leaves in this filling salad.

Serves 4

* 9¾ cups baby spinach
* 2 tablespoons olive oil
* 5½ ounces pancetta, diced
* 10 ounces mixed wild mushrooms, sliced

Dressing

* 1 tablespoon balsamic vinegar
* 1 teaspoon Dijon mustard
* 1 teaspoon maple syrup
* 5 tablespoons olive oil
* salt and pepper, to taste

Toss your salad

To make the dressing, put the vinegar, mustard, maple syrup, and oil in a screw-top jar, season with salt and pepper, screw on the lid, and shake well.

Put the spinach in a salad bowl. Heat the olive oil in a large skillet over medium—high heat. Add the pancetta and cook for 3 minutes, stirring. Add the mushrooms and cook for an additional 3—4 minutes, or until the pancetta is cooked and the mushrooms are tender.

Pour the dressing into the skillet, then immediately add the fried mixture and dressing to the salad bowl. Toss well and serve.

Power pancetta

Pancetta is traditional Italian bacon. It is high in fat, so it is not advisable to eat large amounts of it. However, in limited quantities it will provide a good deal of energy.

Seared beef salad with horseradish dressing

Per serving: 362 cals   12g fat   5g sat fat   35g protein   34g carbs   6.4g fiber

A man-size salad packed with complex carbs for slow-release energy, protein for muscle growth and repair, and iron for healthy blood cells to power you through any exercise program or hectic work schedule.

Serves 4

* 1 pound baby new potatoes, thickly sliced
* 12 cherry tomatoes, halved
* 4 cups baby spinach
* 1 red onion, finely chopped
* 1⅔ cups diced, drained cooked beets in natural juices
* 2 tablespoons balsamic vinegar
* 2 (8-ounce) tenderloin steaks, visible fat removed
* 2 teaspoons olive oil
* 1 teaspoon multicolor peppercorns, coarsely crushed

Dressing

* ½ cup ricotta cheese
* ¼ cup low-fat plain yogurt
* 1–2 teaspoons horseradish sauce
* salt and pepper, to taste

Beef up your salad

Put the potatoes in the top of a steamer, cover, and set over a saucepan of simmering water. Steam for 6–8 minutes, or until tender. Let cool.

Put the cherry tomatoes, spinach, onion, and beets in a salad bowl. Drizzle with the vinegar and toss together.

Preheat a heavy, ridged grill pan over high heat. Brush the steaks with the oil, then sprinkle with the crushed peppercorns. Cook in the hot pan for 2 minutes on each side for medium–rare, 3 minutes on each side for medium, and 4 minutes on each side for well done. Transfer the steaks to a plate and let rest for a few minutes.

To make the dressing, put the ricotta and yogurt in a salad bowl, stir in the horseradish, then season with salt and pepper. Add the potatoes and toss gently together. Divide the spinach salad among four plates, then spoon the potato salad in the center. Thinly slice the steak and arrange it over the top, then serve.

Yes you can enjoy steak!

Beef contains a wide range of minerals, but is particularly rich in iron needed for hemoglobin, the pigment in our red blood cells that carries oxygen around the body, and it works with zinc for maintaining and replicating each person's individual DNA and RNA. Zinc is also essential for normal growth of the body and boosting the immune system.

Sustaining Caesar salad with maple chicken

Per serving: 464 cals 20g fat 5.2g sat fat 52g protein 20g carbs 3.9g fiber

What to eat before you do sports can be a dilemma. You need something that is light but that will give you enough energy to get you through your exercise. This chicken salad offers a good mixture of protein, monounsaturated fats, vegetables, and carbs. Aim to eat at least one hour before exercising, then after exercising start replenishing glycogen stores with a high-carbohydrate, low-fat snack within 30 minutes.

Serves 4

* 4 slices whole-wheat bread, diced
* little low-fat cooking spray
* 2 teaspoon Dijon mustard
* 1 tablespoon maple syrup
* 2 garlic cloves, finely chopped
* 3 tablespoons olive oil
* juice of 1 lemon
* 1 pound boneless, skinless chicken breasts, thinly sliced
* 2 ounces Parmesan cheese
* 4 Romaine lettuce hearts, leaves separated and torn into bite-size pieces

Dressing

* 2 eggs
* 1 teaspoon Worcestershire sauce
* salt and pepper, to taste

Make it chicken tonight

To make croutons, preheat the oven to 400°F. Put the bread on a baking sheet in a single layer, spray with low-fat cooking spray, then bake for 8—10 minutes, turning once, until golden brown and crisp.

Put half the mustard, the maple syrup, half the chopped garlic, 1 tablespoon of olive oil, and the juice of half a lemon in a shallow dish and mix together. Add the chicken and toss to coat. Cover and set aside for no more than 5 minutes.

To make the dressing, put the eggs in a small saucepan, just cover with cold water, then bring to a boil and boil for 1 minute. Drain and cool under cold running water. Crack a little of the shell off each egg, then use a teaspoon to scoop the soft egg into a blender. Add the remaining mustard, garlic and lemon juice and the Worcestershire sauce. Crumble half of the Parmesan and add it to the blender with a little salt and pepper. Blend until smooth, then drizzle in the remaining 2 tablespoons of olive oil with the motor running, and blend again.

Preheat a heavy, ridged grill pan over high heat. Cook the glazed chicken in the hot pan, in batches if necessary, for 8—10 minutes, turning once, or until cooked through. Cut into the middle of a slice to check that the meat is no longer pink and the juices run clear.

Toss the lettuce with half the dressing, then spoon it into four bowls. Thinly shave the remaining Parmesan. Top the salad with the hot chicken and croutons, drizzle with the remaining dressing, and sprinkle with the Parmesan.

Seared beef
salad with
horseradish
dressing
page 54

Sustaining
Caesar salad
with maple
chicken
page 55

Warming new potato & salmon salad

Instead of fattening butter or mayo, this warm potato salad is tossed with a tangy lemon and olive oil dressing, then topped with kale, pea shoots, and salmon for a sustaining main meal.

Serves 4

* 1½ pounds baby new potatoes, halved or thickly sliced if large
* 1 pound salmon fillet
* 1 red onion, thinly sliced
* ½ iceberg lettuce, torn into bite-size pieces
* 1¾ cups shredded kale
* 1¼ cups pea shoots
* salt and pepper, to taste

Dressing

* ¼ cup olive oil
* juice of 1 lemon
* 2 teaspoons honey
* 1 tablespoon capers, drained and chopped

How to make it

Put cold water in the bottom of a steamer, bring to a boil, then add the potatoes and bring back to a boil. Put the salmon in the top of the steamer in a single layer, season with salt and pepper, then put it on the steamer base, cover, and steam for 10 minutes, or until the salmon is cooked. Remove the steamer top and cook the potatoes for an additional 4—5 minutes, or until tender.

Meanwhile, to make the dressing, put the oil, lemon juice, and honey in a salad bowl, mix together well, then stir in the capers and season with salt and pepper.

Add the onion to the dressing, then add the hot potatoes and toss gently together.

Divide the lettuce and kale among four bowls and spoon the potato mixture over them. Flake the salmon into large pieces, discarding any skin and bones, sprinkle over the salad, then top with the pea shoots and serve immediately.

Per serving: 519 cals   29.2g fat   5.3g sat fat   28.3g protein   35.3g carbs   6.2g fiber

Artichoke & prosciutto salad

Per serving: 345 cals 22.4g fat 3.7g sat fat 10.1g protein 27.5g carbs 9g fiber

This is a deliciously fresh, summery salad with a garlicky mustard dressing.
There's no awkward artichoke preparation; simply open a can and enjoy their delicate
taste with protein-rich, wafer-thin slices of prosciutto.

Serves 4

* 12 canned artichoke hearts in oil,
  drained and cut into quarters
* 6 small tomatoes, cut into wedges
* 8 pieces sun-dried tomatoes
  in oil, drained and cut into
  thin strips
* 1½ ounces sliced prosciutto,
  cut into strips
* ¼ cup stoned and halved
  black ripe olives
* 1 cup torn fresh basil,
  plus extra to garnish
* 4 slices crusty white bread,
  to serve

Dressing

* 3 tablespoons olive oil
* 1 tablespoon white wine vinegar
* 1 garlic clove, crushed
* ½ teaspoon mild mustard
* 1 teaspoon honey
* salt and pepper, to taste

Toss your salad

Put the artichokes, tomatoes, sun-dried tomatoes,
prosciutto, olives, and basil in a salad bowl.

To make the dressing, put the oil, vinegar, garlic,
mustard, and honey in a screw-top jar, season with salt
and pepper, screw on the lid, and shake well. Drizzle the
dressing over the salad and toss gently together.

Garnish with the reserved basil and serve immediately
with the crusty bread.

Tuna, lentil & potato energizer salad

Per serving: 554 cals   25.7g fat   3.6g sat fat   37g protein   44g carbs   10.2g fiber

A fresh salad power-packed with lentils, potatoes, and tuna to give you all the energy you need for an afternoon of work or play.

Serves 4

* 1 cup French puy or brown lentils
* 2 tablespoons olive oil, plus extra for brushing
* 10½ ounces baby new potatoes, halved
* 1 Boston or Bibb lettuce
* 4 (4-ounce) tuna steaks
* 16 cherry tomatoes, halved
* 2 cups arugula

Dressing

* ⅓ cup fruity olive oil
* 1 tablespoon balsamic vinegar
* 2 teaspoons red wine vinegar
* 1 teaspoon smooth Dijon mustard
* 1 teaspoon honey

Seaside sensation

Boil the lentils in a saucepan of water for 25 minutes, or according to package directions, until tender. Drain, transfer to a salad bowl, and stir in the olive oil.

Put the potatoes in a saucepan and cover with cold water. Bring to a boil, cover, and simmer for 15 minutes, or until tender. Drain well.

Meanwhile, break the outer leaves off the lettuce and cut the heart into eight pieces. Arrange on four plates.

To make the dressing, put all the ingredients in a screw-top jar, screw on the lid, and shake well.

Preheat a heavy, ridged grill pan over high heat. Brush the tuna with olive oil. Cook it in the hot pan for 3 minutes for rare or 5 minutes for medium, turning once. Transfer it to a plate and cut each steak into six.

Arrange the lentils, tuna, potatoes, and tomatoes over the lettuce, sprinkle with the arugula, and spoon over the dressing. Serve immediately.

Terrific tuna

Tuna is a good source of omega-3 fatty acids, essential fatty acids that are thought to help to reduce the risk of heart disease and arthritis and aid brain and cognitive function.

Warm red lentil salad

Per serving: 336 cals 21g fat 8.6g sat fat 16.4g protein 19.3g carbs 4.3g fiber

Herby dressed lentils make a hearty base for a salad. Their starches are digested and absorbed slowly by the body, giving a sustained energy boost, while their soluble fiber is thought to help reduce blood cholesterol levels.

Serves 4

* 2 tablespoons olive oil
* 2 teaspoons cumin seeds
* 2 garlic cloves, crushed
* ¾-inch piece of fresh ginger, peeled and finely grated
* 1½ cups split red lentils
* 3 cups vegetable stock
* 2 tablespoons coarsely chopped fresh mint
* 2 tablespoons coarsely chopped fresh cilantro
* 2 red onions, thinly sliced
* 7 cups baby spinach
* 1 teaspoon hazelnut oil
* 5½ ounces soft goat cheese
* ¼ cup Greek-style yogurt
* pepper, to taste

Toss your salad

Heat 1 tablespoon of olive oil in a large saucepan over medium heat. Add the cumin, garlic, and ginger and stir-fry for 2 minutes. Stir in the lentils, then add the stock, a ladleful at a time, simmering and stirring occasionally until each ladleful has been absorbed before adding the next one — this will take about 20 minutes in all. Remove from the heat and stir in the herbs.

Meanwhile, heat the remaining 1 tablespoon of olive oil in a skillet over medium—low heat. Add the onions and cook, stirring often, for 10 minutes, or until soft and lightly browned.

Put the spinach and hazelnut oil in a bowl and toss gently together. Divide among four shallow bowls.

Put the goat cheese and yogurt in a small bowl, season with pepper, and mash.

Spoon the lentils onto the spinach, top with the onions, then spoon on the goat cheese and yogurt and serve.

Love your lentils

Lentils are nutritious and economical. They're low in fat and free from cholesterol, but they are a rich source of protein, dietary fiber, the B vitamins, and essential amino acids, and they are a useful source of folic acid.

Roasted tomato whole-wheat pasta salad

Per serving: 473 cals 28.7g fat 5g sat fat 13.8g protein 43g carbs 8.3g fiber

Whole-wheat pasta has long been a favorite energy-boosting base for sportspeople, because exercising muscles rely on carbohydrate as their main source of fuel.

Serves 4

* 1¼ pounds tomatoes in various colors and sizes, halved
* 2 garlic cloves, finely chopped
* ⅓ cup olive oil
* 8 ounces dried whole-wheat pasta, such as quills
* 3 cups baby spinach
* salt and pepper, to taste

Spinach pesto

* 1¼ cups fresh basil, plus extra leaves to garnish
* 3 tablespoons pine nuts
* ¼ cup finely grated fresh Parmesan cheese, plus Parmesan shavings to garnish

Make it now!

Preheat the oven to 325°F. Put the tomatoes in a roasting pan, cut side up, sprinkle with the garlic and 2 tablespoons of olive oil, and season well with salt and pepper. Roast for 40—45 minutes, or until softened and just beginning to brown. Let cool, then chop up any larger ones.

Meanwhile, put the pasta in a large saucepan of boiling water. Bring back to a boil, cover, and simmer according to the package directions, until just tender. Drain into a colander, rinse with cold water, then drain again.

To make the pesto, put all the ingredients in a blender, add 1 cup of the baby spinach and the remaining ¼ cup of olive oil, and process until smooth. Season lightly with salt and pepper.

Put the pasta and pesto in a salad bowl, toss together, then add the remaining spinach and toss again briefly. Add the tomatoes and any pan juices and toss gently. Garnish with the Parmesan shavings and basil leaves and serve.

Carbs for athletes

Athletes need 5—10 g of carbohydrate per 2¼ pounds of body weight each day, compared to the average person who needs 3—5 g.

Pear, celery, blue cheese & walnut salad

Per serving: 382 cals   30.8g fat   7g sat fat   9.2g protein   17g carbs   6.5g fiber

Walnuts have long been revered as a healthy ingredient. In this autumnal salad, they combine with blue cheese to give your body a boost.

Serves 4

* 2 large, juicy, red skin pears
* 4 celery stalks, finely chopped
* squeeze of lemon juice
* 3 tablespoons coarsely chopped fresh flat-leaf parsley
* 5½ cups dark green salad greens, such as arugula, watercress, and baby spinach
* 3½ ounces blue cheese, broken into small chunks
* ¼ cup coarsely chopped walnuts
* sea salt flakes

Dressing

* 1 tablespoon lemon juice
* ¼ cup walnut oil
* ¼ teaspoon pepper

Crunch time

Quarter and core one of the pears, but do not peel it. Slice each quarter lengthwise into thin segments. Put them in a salad bowl, add the celery, and sprinkle with the lemon juice to prevent discoloration.

To make the dressing, quarter and core the second pear. Slice one quarter lengthwise into thin segments and add to the bowl. Peel and coarsely chop the remaining quarters and put them in a blender.

Put the remaining dressing ingredients in the blender and process until smooth.

Add ⅓ cup of the dressing, or just enough to coat, to the salad bowl. Stir in the parsley and season with a pinch of sea salt.

Arrange the salad greens on four plates. Pile the pear and celery mixture on top. Sprinkle with the cheese and walnuts and serve immediately.

Go nuts for walnuts!

Walnuts are rich in monounsaturated fats and are a good source of omega-3 fatty acids. Eating about ¼ cup walnuts per day provides about 75 percent of the omega-3 fatty acids we need.

Tomato & mozzarella superfood salad

Per serving: 377 cals 32g fat 7.3g sat fats 11.8g protein 14g carbs 7g fiber

Superspeedy to put together, this popular salad includes energy-boosting avocado, which is rich in monounsaturated healthy fats and antioxidant vitamins, and has more protein than any other fruit.

Serves 4

* 4 beefsteak tomatoes, cut into thick wedges
* 5½ ounces mozzarella cheese, drained and torn into pieces
* 2 avocados, halved, pitted, peeled, and cut into slices
* few fresh basil leaves, torn
* 20 black ripe olives, stoned

Dressing

* ¼ cup olive oil
* 1½ tablespoons white wine vinegar
* 1 teaspoon whole-grain mustard
* salt and pepper, to taste

Mix it up

Arrange the tomatoes, mozzarella, and avocados in a large serving dish.

To make the dressing, put the olive oil, vinegar, and mustard in a small bowl, mix together, and season with salt and pepper.

Drizzle the dressing over the salad. Sprinkle the basil and olives on top and toss gently together. Serve.

Mmm, mozzarella

Mozzarella is a good source of protein and calcium, for building strong, healthy teeth and bones. It is also high in fat, so it will give you an energy boost, but it should be eaten in moderation.

Avocados

This superfood is thought to be the most nutritionally complete fruit in the world. Containing numerous vitamins and minerals, phytonutrients, and protein, it is a quick, simple nutrient — and energy-booster. The avocado does contain fat, which bumps up its calories, but it is monounsaturated fat, the good kind, which helps maintain healthy cholesterol levels and provides essential fatty acids. Plus, it contains lutein, a natural antioxidant, which is thought to help maintain healthy eyesight and prevent macular degeneration as we age.

High-energy warm egg salad

Per serving: 365 cals 25.2g fat 4.3g sat fat 15.5g protein 21g carbs 5.8g fiber

For all those who say salads aren't filling, this one will prove you wrong! Packed with energy-boosting complex carbs, protein, vitamins, and minerals, this summery lunch will superpower you through the afternoon.

Serves 4

Tapenade

* 1 cup shelled fresh fava beans (about 1 pound unshelled)
* ½ cup stoned green olives
* ¼ cup coarsely chopped fresh flat-leaf parsley
* 2 cups arugula
* 1 small garlic clove, thinly sliced

Salad

* 3 cups baby spinach
* 1¼ cups sliced button mushrooms
* 1 teaspoon white wine vinegar
* 4 eggs
* 4 slices rustic whole-wheat bread
* salt and pepper, to taste

Dressing

* 4 teaspoons balsamic vinegar
* ¼ cup light olive oil, plus extra to serve

How to make it

To make the tapenade, boil the fava beans in a saucepan of water for 5 minutes. Drain and transfer to a food processor. Add the olives, parsley, arugula, and garlic and season with salt and pepper. Process until finely chopped, then keep warm.

Put the spinach and mushrooms in a salad bowl.

To make the dressing, put the vinegar and oil in a bowl, mix together, and season with a little salt and pepper. Drizzle the dressing over the salad and toss gently together. Spoon the salad onto four plates.

Bring a wide saucepan of water to a boil. Add the white wine vinegar and a little salt, then stir and crack in the eggs, one at a time. Simmer gently, until the egg whites are just set but the yolks are still runny.

Meanwhile, toast the bread. Spread the tapenade over the toast and nestle each slice in the salads. Lift the eggs out of the water, using a slotted spoon, then place on top of the toasts. Season with a little extra salt and pepper and sprinkle with a drizzle of olive oil, then serve immediately.

Fava bean-tastic

Fava beans are rich in complex carbohydrates for slow-release energy and soluble fiber. Although fiber does not contain energy or nutrients, it aids digestion and absorption of other foods and encourages healthy bowel movement, so may help to reduce symptoms of irritable bowel syndrome and lower blood cholesterol.

Lovely & light avocado & almond salad

Per serving: 312 cals 25.7g fat 3.1g sat fat 7.4g protein 19.2g carbs 10.5g fiber

Smooth and tasty avocados are flavored with zesty lemon juice, fragrant cilantro, piquant scallions, and hot chile, and given an added crunch with a sprinkling of slivered almonds.

Serves 4

* 2 teaspoons olive oil
* ½ cup slivered almonds
* 1 iceberg lettuce, quartered and torn into bite-size pieces
* 3 avocados, halved, pitted, and peeled
* juice of 2 lemons

Dressing

* ¼ cup low-fat plain yogurt
* 2 scallions, finely chopped
* ¼ teaspoon crushed red pepper flakes
* ⅔ cup finely chopped fresh cilantro (optional)
* salt and pepper, to taste

Amazing almonds

Adding just a spoonful or two of almonds to a salad will help to boost its vitamin E, calcium, and protein levels, and is especially beneficial for vegetarians.

Time to get started

Heat the oil in a skillet over medium heat. Add the almonds and cook for 3–4 minutes, or until golden, stirring often, then let cool.

Put the lettuce in a salad bowl. Slice two of the avocados, put them in a bowl, and squeeze the juice of 1½ lemons over them to prevent discoloration. Transfer the avocados to the salad bowl.

To make the dressing, mash the remaining avocado on a plate with the remaining lemon juice. Mix in the yogurt, scallions, crushed red pepper flakes, and cilantro, if using, and season lightly with salt and pepper.

Spoon the salad into four shallow bowls, sprinkle with the cooked almonds, then spoon the dressing over the salad.

High-energy warm egg salad

page 72

Lovely & light avocado & almond salad

page 73

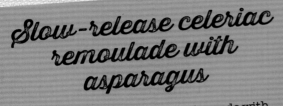

Slow-release celeriac remoulade with asparagus

Remoulade dressing is classically made with mayonnaise and flavored with mustard, pickles, and herbs. For a modern twist, low-fat plain yogurt has been mixed into the dressing to minimize the fat content.

Serves 4

* 1 small head celeriac, peeled and cut into matchsticks
* 4 red-skinned potatoes, peeled and cut into matchsticks
* ½ cup coarsely chopped walnuts
* ⅓ cup drained, chopped pickles
* ¼ cup finely snipped fresh chives
* 16 asparagus spears, trimmed
* 2 tablespoons olive oil
* salt and pepper, to taste

Dressing

* 3 tablespoons light mayonnaise
* 3 tablespoons low-fat plain yogurt
* 2 teaspoons Dijon mustard

Crunch time

Put the celariac and potatoes in a saucepan of boiling water. Bring back to a boil, cover, and simmer for 3—4 minutes, or until tender but still firm. Drain into a colander, rinse with cold water several times to cool quickly, then drain again and transfer to a bowl.

To make the dressing, put the mayonnaise and yogurt in a small bowl. Stir in the mustard and season well with salt and pepper. Pour the dressing over the celeriac and potatoes and toss gently together.

Mix in the walnuts, pickles, and chives. Divide among four shallow bowls.

Preheat a ridged grill pan or skillet over high heat. Put the asparagus and oil in a bowl, season well with salt and pepper, and toss gently together. Cook in the hot pan for 3—4 minutes, or until just tender. Arrange over the salad and serve immediately.

Per serving: 353 cals   19.5g fat   2.2g sat fat   8.3g protein   40.3g carbs   6.9g fiber

Roasted beet & squash salad

Per serving: 505 cals 19.3g fat 2.5g sat fat 10g protein 75g carbs 9g fiber

This nutty-tasting whole-grain salad, topped with vibrant roast beets and butternut squash, can be made the night before and tossed with the beet greens just before you serve it. That means it's perfect for a power-boosting packed lunch!

Serves 4

* 8 raw beets, green stem trimmed, peeled and cut into ¾-inch cubes
* 3 cups ¾-inch butternut squash cubes
* ¼ cup olive oil
* ½ cup long-grain brown rice
* ½ cup red Camargue rice or long-grain brown rice
* ½ cup quick-cook farro
* 3 cups beet greens
* salt and pepper, to taste

Dressing

* 1 tablespoon flaxseed oil
* 2 tablespoons red wine vinegar
* ½ teaspoon smoked hot paprika
* 1 teaspoon fennel seeds, coarsely crushed
* 2 teaspoons tomato paste

How to make it

Preheat the oven to 400°F. Put the beets and squash in a roasting pan, drizzle with half the olive oil, and season with a little salt and pepper. Roast for 30 minutes, or until just tender.

Meanwhile, put the brown rice and Camargue rice in a saucepan of boiling water. Bring back to a boil, then simmer, uncovered, for 15 minutes. Add the farro and cook for an additional 10 minutes, or cook according to the times in the package directions, until all the grains are tender. Drain and rinse, then transfer to a plate.

To make the dressing, put all the ingredients and the remaining 2 tablespoons of olive oil in a screw-top jar, season with salt and pepper, screw on the lid, and shake well. Drizzle the dressing over the rice, then toss.

Spoon the roasted vegetables over the grains and let cool. Toss gently together, then sprinkle with the beet greens and serve immediately.

The brighter the better

The brighter the butternut squash flesh, the more beta-carotene it contains. This is converted into vitamin A, which is vital for healthy eyesight.

Three-bean energy-booster salad

Per serving: 276 cals   13.3g fat   1.6g sat fat   11g protein   29.6g carbs   11.4g fiber

This mighty salad will give you a slow, sustained energy boost. It is made with low-GI foods that are rich in fiber and carbohydrate and take time for the body to break down.

Serves 4

* 2 cups halved green beans
* 1⅓ cups frozen edamame (soybeans) or fava beans
* 1 cup frozen corn kernels
* 2 cups drained and rinsed canned red kidney beans
* 2 tablespoons chia seeds

Dressing

* 3 tablespoons olive oil
* 1 tablespoon red wine vinegar
* 1 teaspoon whole-grain mustard
* 1 teaspoon agave syrup
* 4 teaspoons finely chopped fresh tarragon
* salt and pepper, to taste

Full of beans

Put the green beans, edamame beans, and corn kernels in a saucepan of boiling water. Bring back to a boil, then simmer for 4 minutes, until the green beans are just tender. Drain into a colander, rinse with cold water, then drain again and put in a salad bowl.

Add the kidney beans and chia seeds to the bowl and toss gently together.

To make the dressing, put the oil, vinegar, and mustard in a screw-top jar, then add the agave syrup and tarragon, and season with salt and pepper. Screw on the lid and shake well. Drizzle the dressing over the salad, toss gently together, and serve immediately.

Three cheers for chia

Originally eaten by the Mayans and Aztecs, chia seeds are rich in protein, which helps to build and repair muscles. They are the richest combined plant source of omega-3, -6, and -9 fatty acids. A tablespoon of chia seeds provides 5 g of fiber; a woman should aim for 25 g of fiber per day and a man 38 g.

Chunky avocado & corn salad

Per serving: 188 cals 12.5g fat 1.7g sat fat 3.3g protein 19.6g carbs 4.9g fiber

A light-tasting mix of creamy avocado, crunchy bell peppers, corn, and kale, flavored with fresh cilantro and tangy lime for a concentrated energy boost to see you through a busy afternoon.

Serves 4

* 1⅓ cups frozen corn kernels
* 1 large avocado, halved, pitted, peeled, and cut into cubes
* 10 cherry tomatoes, quartered
* ½ red onion, finely chopped
* 1 small green bell pepper, halved, seeded, and cut into small chunks
* ½ cup shredded kale
* ½ cup coarsely chopped fresh cilantro

Dressing

* finely grated zest and juice of 1 lime
* 2 tablespoons olive oil
* salt and pepper, to taste

How to make it

Put the corn kernels in a saucepan of boiling water. Bring back to a boil, then simmer for 3 minutes. Drain into a colander, rinse with cold water, drain again, then transfer to a salad bowl.

To make the dressing, put the lime zest and juice and oil in a screw-top jar, season with salt and pepper, screw on the lid, and shake well.

Add the avocado, tomatoes, onion, green bell pepper, kale, and cilantro to the salad bowl. Drizzle the dressing over the salad and toss gently together. Spoon into four bowls and serve immediately.

Sweet corn

Naturally sweet and packed with complex carbs and fiber, corn provides a sustained and stable energy boost to help us avoid mood swings.

Health

High-fiber chicken salad

Per serving: 694 cals 20g fat 3.2g sat fat 46.3g protein 79.7g carbs 5.6g fiber

Capture the flavors and colors of Morocco with this spicy brown rice salad flecked with jewel-like diced dried apricots and glistening raisins, and tossed with health-boosting green kale.

Serves 4

* 1⅓ cups brown rice
* 2 teaspoons tomato paste
* 1 pound skinless, boneless chicken breasts
* ⅔ cup diced dried apricots
* ⅓ cup raisins
* ½ pickled lemon, drained and finely chopped
* 1 small red onion, finely chopped
* 1¼ cups shredded kale
* 3 tablespoons pine nuts, toasted

Dressing

* 2 teaspoons harissa
* ¼ cup olive oil
* juice of 1 lemon
* salt and pepper, to taste

How to make it

Put the rice in a pan of boiling water. Bring back to a boil, then simmer for 25—30 minutes, or according to the package directions, until tender. Drain and transfer to a bowl.

Meanwhile, to make the dressing, put the harissa, oil, and lemon juice in a screw-top jar, season with salt and pepper, screw on the lid, and shake well.

Spoon 2 tablespoons of the dressing into a bowl and mix in the tomato paste. Preheat the broiler to high and line the broiler pan with aluminum foil. Put the chicken on the foil in a single layer. Brush some of the tomato dressing over the chicken, then broil for 15—18 minutes, or until golden and cooked through, turning the meat and brushing it with the remaining tomato dressing halfway through cooking. Cut through the middle of a breast to check that the meat is no longer pink and that any juices run clear and are piping hot. Cover and let cool.

Drizzle the remaining dressing over the rice in the bowl. Add the dried apricots, raisins, pickled lemon, and onion, then toss gently together and let cool. Add the kale and pine nuts to the salad and stir. Thinly slice the chicken, arrange it over the top, and serve.

Health-giving rice

Rice is an important source of protein and energy. Brown rice has less of the bran removed, meaning that it retains far more vital nutrients and fiber than white rice, which has more of the bran removed. Homeopaths believe that rice can help treat digestive disorders, from indigestion to diverticulitis.

Brain-boosting ruby couscous salad with grilled chicken

Per serving: 521 cals 16.5g fat 2g sat fat 45.8g protein 48.4g carbs 5.2g fiber

This salad looks good and does you good, too! The beets turn everything a deep vibrant red and glisten with the gemlike pomegranate seeds.

Serves 4

* 1 cup giant whole-wheat couscous
* 1¼ cups diced, drained cooked beets in natural juices
* 1 small red onion, finely chopped
* 8 cherry tomatoes, halved
* 1 pomegranate, halved, with seeds removed and reserved
* juice of 2 lemons
* 2 tablespoons flaxseed oil
* 2 tablespoons olive oil
* 4 teaspoons tomato paste
* 2 tablespoons coarsely chopped fresh mint
* 1 teaspoon black peppercorns, coarsely crushed
* 1 pound skinless, boneless chicken breasts, sliced
* salt and pepper, to taste

Create your salad

Put the couscous in a saucepan of boiling water. Bring back to a boil, then simmer for 6—8 minutes, until just tender, or according to package directions. Drain into a strainer, rinse with cold water, then transfer to a salad bowl. Add the beets, onion, tomatoes, and pomegranate seeds.

To make the dressing, put the juice of one lemon, the flaxseed oil, half the olive oil, and half the tomato paste in a screw-top jar, season with salt and pepper, screw on the lid, and shake well. Drizzle the dressing over the salad, then sprinkle on the mint and toss together.

Put the remaining lemon juice, olive oil, and tomato paste and the crushed peppercorns in a clean plastic bag, twist, and shake well. Add the chicken, seal, then shake until the chicken is evenly coated.

Preheat a ridged grill pan over high heat. Cook the chicken (in batches if necessary) in the hot pan for 10 minutes, turning once or twice, until cooked through. Cut through the middle of a slice to check that the meat is no longer pink and any juices run clear and are piping hot. Arrange over the salad and serve.

Brain-boosting beets

The high levels of nitrates in beet may help slow down the progression of dementia. When the pigment betacyanin, which gives beet their color, combines with carotenoids and flavonoids, it may help reduce the oxidation of LDL cholesterol, so protecting artery walls and reducing the risk of heart disease and stroke.

Pick-me-up shrimp & white bean salad

Per serving: 408 cals 19.5g fat 3.1g sat fat 23.5g protein 35g carbs 3.4g fiber

Forget about student-style sloppy joes. This stylish salad mixes canned navy beans with shrimp and gives them a tangy lemon and parsley dressing for a fresh-tasting, protein-boosting alternative.

Serves 4

* 2 cups rinsed, drained canned navy beans or other white beans
* ½ red onion, finely chopped
* 1 celery stalk, finely chopped
* 10½ ounces cooked, peeled large shrimp, with tails intact, thawed if frozen
* 1 garlic clove, finely chopped
* juice of 1 lemon
* ⅓ cup extra virgin olive oil
* 2 tablespoons coarsely chopped fresh flat-leaf parsley, plus extra whole leaves, to garnish
* 4 thick slices of country-style or sourdough bread
* ½ cup halved baby plum tomatoes
* salt and pepper, to taste

Crunch time

Put the beans, onion, celery, shrimp, and garlic in a large, shallow bowl. Add the lemon juice, 2 tablespoons of the oil, and the parsley. Season lightly with salt and pepper, stir well, then cover and set aside.

Preheat a ridged grill pan over high heat. Brush the bread with some of the remaining oil. Cook in the hot pan for 2—3 minutes on each side, or until golden. Transfer to four plates.

Gently stir the tomatoes into the salad. Pile the salad onto the hot toasts. Drizzle the rest of the olive oil over the top, garnish with the whole parsley leaves, season with a little more pepper, and serve.

The power of white beans

White beans offer terrific health benefits. They are loaded with antioxidants and provide a good supply of detoxifying molybdenum. They are also a good source of fiber and protein and rank low on the glycemic index. They produce alpha-amylase inhibitors, which help regulate fat storage in the body.

Vitamin B-boosting feta, mint & strawberry salad

Per serving: 354 cals   30g fat   12g sat fat   11.3g protein   12g carbs   3.2g fiber

Strawberries are a great way to boost your vitamin C, which is needed daily by the body. Their natural sweetness works well with the saltiness of the feta cheese and crispness of the blanched beans in this salad.

Serves 4

* 2½ cups green beans
* 1½ cups hulled and halved strawberries
* 1 tablespoon shelled pistachio nuts
* ¼ cup fresh mint
* 1⅔ cups feta cheese chunks
* pepper, to taste

Dressing

* 1 tablespoon raspberry vinegar
* 1 teaspoon agave syrup
* 1 teaspoon Dijon mustard
* ¼ cup olive oil
* pinch of salt

For your salad

To make the dressing, put the vinegar, agave syrup, mustard, and salt in a bowl and stir until smooth. Slowly pour in the oil, whisking constantly.

Put the green beans in a saucepan of boiling water. Bring back to a boil, then simmer for 5 minutes, or until just tender. Drain into a colander, rinse with cold water, then drain again and put into a salad bowl. Add the strawberries, pistachio nuts, and mint. Drizzle with enough dressing to coat lightly, then toss gently together.

Sprinkle the feta over the salad, season well with pepper, and serve immediately.

Super strawberries

Strawberries have more vitamin C than any other red berries and so have good antiviral and antibacterial properties. They are rich in beta-carotene. Their natural fruit sugars also give the body an energy boost.

Ratatouille & bean salad

Per serving: 167 cals 4.6g fat 0.6g sat fat 8.4g protein 23g carbs 9g fiber

This healthy, high-fiber salad can be eaten slightly warm and then any leftovers refrigerated and taken to work the next day in a lunch bag, with the greens in a separate plastic bag to keep them fresh.

Serves 4

* ✳ 1 tablespoon olive oil
* ✳ 1 red onion, coarsely chopped
* ✳ 1 red bell pepper, halved, seeded, and cut into chunks
* ✳ 1 green bell pepper, halved, seeded, and cut into chunks
* ✳ 1 orange bell pepper, halved, seeded, and cut into chunks
* ✳ 2 garlic cloves, finely chopped
* ✳ 3 tomatoes, skinned and coarsely chopped
* ✳ 1 tablespoon tomato paste
* ✳ ¼ teaspoon smoked hot paprika
* ✳ 2 stems of fresh rosemary
* ✳ 2 zucchini, cut into chunks
* ✳ 2 cups rinsed, drained canned cannellini beans
* ✳ 2 cups mixed baby salad greens, including arugula, red Swiss chard, mustard greens, or mizuna
* ✳ 1 tablespoon balsamic vinegar
* ✳ salt and pepper, to taste

Mix it up

Heat the oil in a saucepan over medium heat. Add the onion and sauté gently for 5 minutes, stirring, until softened and just beginning to brown. Add the bell peppers, garlic, and tomatoes, then stir in the tomato paste and paprika.

Add the rosemary and season well with salt and pepper. Cover and simmer for 10 minutes. Stir in the zucchini and cook for 5 minutes, until just beginning to soften but still bright green.

Remove the pan from the heat and stir in the cannellini beans. Season with salt and pepper and discard the rosemary. Transfer to a salad bowl and let cool.

When ready to serve, toss the baby greens in the balsamic vinegar and sprinkle over the salad. Serve in shallow bowls.

Beet, spinach & Brie nutrient-boosting salad

Per serving: 459 cals   39.8g fat   12g sat fat   15g protein   14g carbs   4.1g fiber

Packed with vitamins and minerals, this vibrant salad is topped with meltingly soft Brie and toasted walnuts, and it's so delicious you'll be coming back for more.

Serves 4

* 6 cups baby spinach
* 2 raw beets, green stem trimmed, peeled, and very thinly sliced
* 1¼ cups ready-to-eat bean sprouts
* 6 ounces Brie, diced

Dressing

* ¾ cup walnut pieces
* 1 teaspoon fennel seeds, coarsely crushed
* ¼ cup rice bran oil
* 2 tablespoons red wine vinegar
* 2 teaspoons brown rice syrup
* salt and pepper, to taste

Give it a whirl

Put the spinach, beets, and bean sprouts into a salad bowl.

To make the dressing, preheat a skillet over medium heat. Put the walnuts and fennel seeds in the hot pan and cook for 2–3 minutes, until lightly toasted. Remove from the heat and add the rice bran oil, then let cool for 5 minutes.

Strain the cooled oil into a screw-top jar, add the vinegar and rice syrup, and season with salt and pepper. Screw on the lid and shake well. Drizzle the dressing over the salad and toss gently together.

Sprinkle the Brie over the salad and spoon the walnuts and fennel on top. Serve immediately.

Health benefits of Brie

There's no getting away from the fact that Brie contains fat, but the fat content is surprisingly lower than that of hard cheeses, such as Gruyère or Cheddar, although Brie looks so soft and creamy. Compare 28 g fat, of which 17.4 g is saturated fat, per 3½ ounces of Brie to 33 g fat, of which 19 g is saturated fat, per 3½ ounces of Gruyère.

Ratatouille &
bean salad

page 92

Beet, spinach &
Brie nutrient-
boosting salad

page 93

Fattoush

This brightly colored Lebanese salad is packed with the fresh taste of lemon, mint, and cilantro and topped with warm pieces of grilled pita bread.

Serves 4

* 1 small red bell pepper, halved, seeded, and diced
* 1 small yellow bell pepper, halved, seeded, and diced
* 1 small green bell pepper, halved, seeded, and diced
* 1 cucumber, peeled, halved lengthwise, seeded, and diced
* 2 scallions, finely chopped
* ½ cup finely chopped fresh mint
* ½ cup finely chopped fresh cilantro
* 2 pita breads
* ½ cup crumbled feta cheese

Dressing

* juice of 1 lemon
* 3 tablespoons olive oil
* ½ teaspoon cumin seeds, coarsely crushed
* 1 garlic clove, finely chopped
* pepper, to taste

How to make it

Put the bell peppers, cucumber, and scallions in a salad bowl, sprinkle with the herbs, and toss gently together.

To make the dressing, put the lemon juice, oil, cumin, and garlic in a screw-top jar, season with a little pepper, screw on the lid, and shake well. Drizzle the dressing over the salad and toss gently together, then spoon into four bowls.

Preheat a ridged grill pan over medium heat. Cook the pita breads in the hot pan for 1½ minutes on each side, until hot and puffy. Transfer to a plate and cut into small pieces. Sprinkle the pita and feta over the salad and serve immediately.

Per serving: 263 cals 15.3g fat 4.7g sat fat 7.2g protein 25g carbs 3.3g fiber

High-fiber green lentil salad

Per serving: 429 cals 17.6g fat 4.2g sat fat 23.5g protein 44.6g carbs 6.9g fiber

Salads don't need to be enjoyed only when the weather is hot. This robust, earthy lentil salad can be rustled up quickly after work, and because it is served just warm, it makes a great dish for cooler fall days.

Serves 4

* 3½ cups vegetable stock
* 2 bay leaves
* 1 cinnamon stick, halved
* 2½ leeks
* 2 cups rinsed, drained dried green lentils
* 3 tablespoons olive oil
* 2 garlic cloves, finely chopped
* 4 eggs
* 2 tablespoons drained, chopped capers
* 3 cups baby spinach
* ½ cup coarsely chopped fresh flat-leaf parsley

Dressing

* 2 tablespoons red wine vinegar
* 1 teaspoon Dijon mustard
* salt and pepper, to taste

Toss it together

Put the stock, bay, and cinnamon in a saucepan and bring just to a boil. Cut a 3-inch piece from the white bottom of one of the leeks and add it and the lentils to the pan. Cover and simmer for 25 minutes, or according to the package directions, until the lentils are tender and nearly all the stock has been absorbed. Add a little boiling water during cooking, if needed. Drain the lentils, then transfer to a salad bowl and discard the cooked leek, bay, and cinnamon.

Meanwhile, thinly slice the rest of the leeks. Heat 1 tablespoon of olive oil in a skillet over medium heat. Add the sliced leeks and the garlic and sauté for 3—4 minutes, stirring, until just beginning to soften. Remove from the heat and let cool.

Put the eggs in a saucepan and pour in enough cold water to cover them by ½ inch. Bring to a boil, then reduce the heat and boil for 8 minutes. Drain immediately, cool quickly under cold running water, then peel and cut into quarters.

To make the dressing, put the vinegar, remaining 2 tablespoons of oil, and the mustard in a screw-top jar, season with salt and pepper, screw on the lid, and shake well. Drizzle the dressing over the lentils and toss gently together. Top with the sliced leeks, capers, and spinach. Arrange the hard-boiled eggs over the salad, sprinkle with the parsley, and serve warm.

Oh-so-good-for-you broccolini salad

Per serving: 232 cals   11.1g fat   1.4g sat fat   6.2g protein   29g carbs   6.5g fiber

Broccoli, including broccolini (or baby broccoli) is one of the main superfoods. It contains sulforaphane, which is thought to have a powerful anticancer effect, especially against tumors of the digestive tract, lungs, and prostate gland. Steam broccoli where possible, because boiling halves the amount of vitamin C it contains.

Serves 4

* 7 ounces broccolini
* 2½ cups shredded red cabbage
* ¾ cup drained, cooked beet matchsticks (canned in their natural juices)
* 2 tablespoons dried cranberries
* 3 tablespoons balsamic vinegar
* 1 tablespoon sunflower seeds
* 1 tablespoon flaxseeds

Croutons

* 2 tablespoons olive oil
* 3 slices rustic whole-grain bread, torn into small pieces

Crunch time

Put the broccolini in the top of a steamer, cover, and set over a saucepan of simmering water. Steam for 3–5 minutes, or until tender. Cool under cold running water, then cut the stems in half and the larger stems in half again lengthwise, and transfer them to a salad bowl.

Add the red cabbage, beet matchsticks, and dried cranberries to the salad bowl.

To make the croutons, heat the oil in a skillet over medium heat, add the bread, and cook for 3–4 minutes, stirring, until beginning to brown. Add the sunflower seeds and flaxseeds and cook for 2–3 minutes, until lightly toasted. Drizzle the balsamic vinegar over the salad and toss gently together. Sprinkle with the croutons and seeds and serve.

Go to the dark side ...

The darker the broccoli florets, either purple, green, or deep blue-green, the higher the amount of beta-carotene and vitamin C. Broccoli also contains folates, iron, and potassium.

Mineral-boosting three-seed salad

Per serving: 212 cals 14.6g fat 2g sat fat 6.7g protein 16g carbs 4.7g fiber

Protein- and mineral-rich seeds are blended with yogurt and lemon for a hummus-style dressing that tastes delicious over spinach and celery leaves.

Serves 4

* 4 cups baby spinach
* ½ oakleaf lettuce, leaves separated and torn into bite-size pieces
* 2 celery stalks, sliced
* small handful of celery leaves, coarsely chopped, plus a few extra to garnish
* 1 cup blueberries
* juice of 2 lemons
* salt and pepper, to taste

Dressing

* 2 tablespoons sesame seeds, toasted, plus extra to garnish
* 2 tablespoons sunflower seeds
* 2 tablespoons flaxseeds
* 1 garlic clove, sliced
* 2 tablespoons olive oil
* ⅔ cup low-fat plain yogurt

How to make it

Put the spinach and lettuce in a salad bowl. Sprinkle with the celery, celery leaves, and blueberries. Drizzle the juice of one lemon over the salad, season with salt and pepper, and toss gently together.

To make the dressing, put the sesame seeds, sunflower seeds, and flaxseeds in a blender. Add the garlic, oil, and juice of the remaining lemon juice and season with salt and pepper. Blend until the seeds are finely ground, then scrape down the sides of the jar and add the yogurt. Blend again briefly until you have a fine paste.

Divide the salad among four plates and add a generous spoonful of the dressing to the center of each plate. Garnish with a few extra sesame seeds and celery leaves and serve.

Seeds of good health

Flaxseeds have the most minerals of all the seeds, containing calcium, magnesium, phosphorus, potassium, and zinc. If they are eaten whole, they tend not to be absorbed by the body, but if they are blended, they are well absorbed. Sunflower and sesame seeds are good sources of vitamin E, and sesame seeds also contain calcium. All the seeds contain protein and fiber and are high in unsaturated fats.

Protective Indian spiced slaw

Per serving: 193 cals 12g fat 1.6g sat fat 7.2g protein 17g carbs 4.2g fiber

Forget about mayonnaise, this extra-healthy coleslaw is made with low-fat plain yogurt instead, then spiced with garam masala and turmeric for an exotic twist.

Serves 4

* ⅔ cup low-fat plain yogurt
* 2 cups shredded red cabbage
* ½ cup shredded kale
* 1 red Pippin or other sweet crisp apple, cored, and shredded
* 1 large carrot, shredded
* salt and pepper, to taste

Topping

* 2 tablespoons pumpkin seeds
* 2 tablespoons sunflower seeds
* 2 tablespoons slivered almonds
* 1½ teaspoons garam masala
* ½ teaspoon turmeric
* 1 tablespoon sunflower oil

Mix it up

To make the topping, preheat a skillet over medium heat. Put the pumpkin seeds, sunflower seeds, almonds, ½ teaspoon of garam masala, and ¼ teaspoon of turmeric in the hot pan and pour in the oil. Cook for 3—4 minutes, stirring often, until the almonds are golden brown. Leave to cool.

To make the dressing, put the yogurt and remaining 1 teaspoon of garam masala and ¼ teaspoon of turmeric in a large bowl, season with salt and pepper and stir well.

Add the cabbage, kale, apple, and carrot to the bowl and toss gently together. Divide the salad among four bowls, sprinkle the topping over it, and serve.

Boost your immunity

Red cabbage, kale, and carrots are all high in antioxidants, and the vitamin C-rich apples will help boost your immune system.

Immune-boosting summer vegetable carpaccio

Per serving: 359 cals   21.4g fat   2.8g sat fat   8.8g protein   36.8g carbs   10.6g fiber

The secret of this pretty, vibrant salad is to cut the vegetables as thinly as possible so that you can almost see through the slices. A mandoline is perfect for this, but be careful of your fingers. If you don't have one, your favorite knife will work equally well, but it will take a little longer.

Serves 4

Hummus

* 2 cups rinsed, drained canned chickpeas
* 1 garlic clove, finely chopped
* 1 tablespoon chia seeds
* 2 tablespoons sesame seeds, toasted
* juice of 1 lemon
* 2 tablespoons olive oil
* salt and pepper, to taste

Salad

* 16 asparagus spears, thinly sliced lengthwise
* 2 carrots, very thinly sliced lengthwise
* 1 raw red beet, green stem trimmed, peeled and very thinly sliced, any tiny leaves reserved
* 1 raw golden beet, green stem trimmed, peeled and very thinly sliced, any tiny leaves reserved
* 5 yellow cherry tomatoes, thinly sliced
* 3 tomatoes, thinly sliced

Dressing

* juice of ½ lemon
* 3 tablespoons olive oil
* 1 teaspoon Dijon mustard

Crunch time

To make the hummus, put the chickpeas, garlic, chia seeds, and sesame seeds in a food processor. Add the lemon juice and oil and season well with salt and pepper. Process until you have a coarse, spreadable paste.

Put the asparagus, carrots, beets, yellow cherry tomatoes, and salad tomatoes in a salad bowl.

To make the dressing, put the lemon juice, oil, and mustard in a screw-top jar, season with a little salt and pepper, screw on the lid, and shake well. Drizzle the dressing over the salad and toss gently together.

To serve, spoon the hummus into the center of four plates, then spread into a thin circle, using the back of the spoon. Pile the salad on top, garnish with the reserved tiny beet leaves, and serve.

Wheat berry & goji berry salad

Per serving: 420 cals 22.8g fat 3.1g sat fat 12.8g protein 49g carbs 10g fiber

Wheat berries are small, whole-grain wheat kernels with all the bran, germ, and everything in-between. They are packed with complex carbohydrates, the B vitamins, vitamin E, a range of minerals, and fiber. With a great, nutty taste, they make a healthy alternative to rice in salads.

Serves 4

* 2½ cups vegetable stock
* ¾ cup wheat berries
* ⅓ cup dried goji berries
* 2 carrots
* 2 cups shredded kale

Dressing

* ½ cup coarsely chopped hazelnuts
* 2 tablespoons sesame seeds
* 2 tablespoons sunflower seeds
* 2 tablespoons soy sauce
* 2 tablespoons sesame oil
* juice of ½ orange

Time to get started

Bring the stock to a boil in a saucepan, add the wheat berries, and simmer for 25 minutes, or until just tender. Drain off and discard the stock, spoon the wheat berries into a salad bowl, and stir in the goji berries.

To make the dressing, dry-fry the hazelnuts, sesame seeds, and sunflower seeds in a skillet over medium—high heat for 3—4 minutes, or until just turning golden brown. Remove from the heat, stir in the soy sauce, then let cool for 1 minute. Mix in the sesame oil and orange juice. Spoon half over the wheat berries, toss together, then let cool.

Shave the carrots into long, thin ribbons, using a swivel-blade vegetable peeler, and add to the salad bowl. Add the kale, toss gently together, then spoon the remaining dressing over it and serve.

Gorgeous goji berries

These tiny Himalayan red berries are rich in beta-carotene and are a good source of the B vitamins and antioxidants. Some people believe they may even help reduce cellulite.

Immune-boosting
summer vegetable
carpaccio

page 104

Wheat berry
& goji berry
salad

page 105

Spinach & tomato salad with roasted garlic croutons

When it's roasted, garlic loses its pungency and has a mild, almost sweet flavor.

Serves 4

* 1 garlic bulb, halved crosswise
* ⅓ cup olive oil
* 3 cups baby spinach
* 3 cups mixed salad greens
* 12 cherry tomatoes, halved
* 4 slices whole-wheat French bread

Dressing

* 2 tablespoons pumpkin seeds
* 2 tablespoons sunflower seeds
* 2 tablespoons flaxseeds, coarsely crushed
* ¼ teaspoon smoked hot paprika
* 4 teaspoons balsamic vinegar
* salt and pepper, to taste

Crunch time

Preheat the oven to 350°F. Put the garlic halves into a piece of crumpled aluminum foil and place in a small roasting pan. Drizzle with 1 tablespoon of olive oil and roast for 20 minutes, or until the cloves are golden and softened.

To make the dressing, dry-fry the pumpkin seeds, sunflower seeds, and flaxseeds in a skillet over medium—high heat for 3—4 minutes, or until just turning golden brown. Remove from the heat, stir in the smoked paprika and ¼ cup of olive oil, then let cool.

When the dressing is cool, add the balsamic vinegar and season with salt and pepper.

Put the spinach and salad greens in a salad bowl, then sprinkle with the tomatoes. Drizzle with the dressing and toss gently together, then divide among four plates.

Toast the bread on both sides. Scoop the soft garlic cloves from their papery casing, then finely chop the flesh until you have a coarse paste. Spread thinly over the toasts and season with a little salt and pepper. Arrange on the top of the salads, drizzle with the remaining olive oil, and serve.

Per serving: 378 cals   29g fat   3.9g sat fat   7.9g protein   24.6g carbs   5g fiber

Three-berry bonanza

Per serving: 169 cals   10.8g fat   0.7g sat fat   2.2g protein   17g carbs   4g fiber

Serve this fresh fruit salad as a side dish or appetizer. The clean, tangy flavors will wake up your taste-buds and it will boost the health of your immune system.

Serves 4

* 1 small head of radicchio, leaves separated and torn into bite-size pieces
* ½ oakleaf or brown-tinged lollo rosso lettuce, leaves separated and torn into bite-size pieces
* ¼ cup dried goji berries
* 1 cup raspberries
* ¾ cup blueberries

Dressing

* 3 tablespoons hemp oil
* juice of ½ lemon
* 1 teaspoon brown rice syrup
* salt and pepper, to taste

Hurray for hemp

Hemp oil contains more omega-3, -6, and -9 fatty acids (the good polyunsaturated fats) than any other oil used for cooking.

How to make it

Put the radicchio and oakleaf lettuce in a salad bowl. Add the goji berries, raspberries, and blueberries and toss gently together.

To make the dressing, put the hemp oil, lemon juice, and brown rice syrup in a screw-top jar, season with a little salt and pepper, screw on the lid, and shake well. Drizzle the dressing over the salad, and toss gently together. Spoon into four shallow bowls and serve.

Green goddess

Per serving: 250 cals   17.7g fat   2g sat fat   10g protein   11g carbs   6.5g fiber

A pretty, delicate salad from a summer garden. Garnish with a few tiny edible herb or viola flowers, or nasturtium or marigold petals, if you prefer.

Serves 4

* 1⅓ cups frozen edamame (soybeans), or shelled fava beans
* 1 cup green beans
* 8 cups (about 1 pound) peas in pods, any tiny flat pods halved, the rest shelled
* ¾ cup pea shoots
* 1½ cups ready-to-eat alfalfa sprouts, radish sprouts, or other sprouts

Dressing

* 2 tablespoons rice bran oil
* 2 tablespoons olive oil
* juice of 1 lime
* 1 teaspoon agave syrup
* ¾-inch piece of fresh ginger, peeled and finely grated
* salt and pepper, to taste

How to make it

Bring a saucepan of water to a boil, add the edamame and green beans, and simmer for 2 minutes. Add any pea pods and simmer for another 1 minute. Drain into a strainer, cool under cold running water, and drain again. Transfer to a salad bowl and sprinkle with the raw peas.

To make the dressing, put the rice bran oil, olive oil, lime juice, agave syrup, and ginger in a screw-top jar, season with a little salt and pepper, screw on the lid, and shake well.

Drizzle the dressing over the salad and toss gently together. Top with the pea shoots and sprouts and serve immediately.

Perfect peas

Serving the peas raw means that you don't sacrifice any vitamin C or thiamine content, a proportion of which is lost during cooking because these vitamins are water-soluble.

Sprouting seeds

Think of bean sprouts, including those sprouted from other seeds, as nutritional powerhouses. As the seeds germinate and begin to sprout, their natural nutrients multiply to meet the growing needs of the young shoots. This makes them a good way to add a range of antioxidants and immune-boosting vitamins, minerals, and protein to a salad. As the seeds sprout, so the plant enzymes increase, which also aids digestion. Choose from alfalfa, adzuki, beet, broccoli, or red clover seeds for a colorful, fresh-tasting, low-priced, all-year-round addition to any salad. Children younger than five, older adults, pregnant women, and those with weakened immune systems are particularly vulnerable to the bacteria that may be present on sprouts, so it is recommended that they should not eat raw sprouts and should only eat cooked sprouts if they have been thoroughly cooked. Buy prepacked sprouting seeds from the shops or grow them from a kit following the manufacturer's instructions, and wash them well before eating.

Cholesterol-lowering multigrain salad

Per serving: 384 cals   17.6g fat   3g sat fat   9.8g protein   45g carbs   8g fiber

There is evidence that adding plenty of soluble fiber from grains or whole foods, such as wild rice, bulgur wheat, and quinoa, to the diet lowers blood cholesterol levels because the gumlike substance binds with cholesterol and carries it out of the body.

Serves 4

* 3 cups vegetable stock
* ¼ cup wild rice
* ¾ cup bulgur wheat
* ⅔ cup quinoa
* ¼ cup olive oil
* 2 zucchini, sliced lengthwise
* 4 scallions, halved lengthwise
* juice ½ lemon
* 1 teaspoon cumin seeds, coarsely crushed
* ½ cup coarsely chopped fresh flat-leaf parsley
* 1½ cups ready-to-eat alfalfa sprouts, radish sprouts, or other sprouts
* salt and pepper, to taste

Dressing

* finely grated zest and juice of ½ unwaxed lemon
* finely grated zest and juice of 1 lime
* 1 teaspoon honey

To make this salad

Bring the stock to a boil in a saucepan, add the rice, and simmer for 5 minutes. Add the bulgur wheat and simmer for an additional 5 minutes. Add the quinoa and simmer for 10—12 minutes, or prepare according to the times on the package directions, until all the grains are tender. Drain off and discard the stock and spoon the grains into a salad bowl.

To make the dressing, put the lemon and lime zest and juices, honey, and 2 tablespoons of olive oil in a screw-top jar, season with salt and pepper, screw on the lid, and shake well. Drizzle over the grains, toss gently together, then let cool.

Meanwhile, mix the zucchini and scallions with the remaining olive oil, the lemon juice, and cumin and season with a little salt and pepper.

Preheat a ridged grill pan over high heat. Cook the zucchini and scallions in the hot pan for 1—2 minutes on each side, or until browned. Transfer to a plate and let cool. Serve the grains on four plates and top with the griddled vegetables. Garnish with the parsley and sprouts.

Fiber facts

Soluble dietary fiber stabilizes blood sugar levels by slowing down the rate at which glucose is absorbed by the body, so helping to avoid drops in energy and mood swings.

Slimming

Thanksgiving turkey & cranberry salad

Per serving: 327 cals 2.6g fat 0.6g sat fat 22.5g protein 53.3g carbs 4.2g fiber

Enjoy all the flavor of Thanksgiving, but in a salad. Why not take this to a bring-and-share supper, or pack individual portions for a work lunch — put the arugula in a separate bag and add just before serving so that it stays crisp.

Serves 4

* 1 cup long-grain brown rice
* ¼ cup wild rice
* 9 ounces turkey breast slices
* ⅓ cup dried cranberries
* 3 scallions, finely chopped
* 2 tomatoes, diced
* 1 small red bell pepper, halved, seeded, and cut into chunks
* 2 cups arugula
* 1½ ounces wafer-thin lean ham, cut into strips
* salt and pepper, to taste

Dressing

* 1½ tablespoons cranberry sauce
* 1½ tablespoons sherry vinegar
* finely grated zest and juice of 1 small unwaxed lemon
* 1 level teaspoon Dijon mustard

Toss it together

Put cold water in the bottom of a steamer, bring to a boil, then add the brown rice and wild rice and bring back to a boil. Put the turkey in the top of the steamer in a single layer, season with salt and pepper, then put it on the steamer base, cover, and steam for 15 minutes, or until the turkey is cooked; cut into the middle of a slice to check that the meat is no longer pink and that the juices are clear and piping hot. Remove the steamer top and cook the rice for an additional 5—10 minutes, or according to the package directions, until tender.

Dice the turkey and put it in a bowl. Add the cranberries. Drain and rinse the rice, then add to the bowl.

To make the dressing, put the cranberry sauce in a small saucepan, and place over low heat until just melted. Remove from the heat, then add the vinegar, lemon zest and juice, and mustard, and season with salt and pepper. Whisk together until smooth, then drizzle the dressing over the salad and let cool.

Add the scallions, tomatoes, and red bell pepper to the salad. Toss gently together, then divide among four plates. Top with the arugula and ham and serve.

Steak salad with light Thousand Island dressing

Per serving: 287 cals 8g fat 2.8g sat fat 35.7g protein 18.4g carbs 4.6g fiber

This salad is traditionally made with mayonnaise, but a light Thousand Island dressing tastes every bit as good.

Serves 4

* 3 slices whole-wheat seeded bread, cut into cubes
* little low-fat cooking spray
* 1 cup halved green beans
* 2 cups broccoli florets and sliced stems
* 2 (8-ounce) tenderloin steaks, visible fat removed
* ½ iceberg lettuce, leaves separated and torn into bite-size pieces
* ½ cucumber, halved lengthwise, seeded and sliced

Dressing

* 1 cup low-fat plain yogurt
* 2 teaspoons tomato paste
* 2 teaspoons Worcestershire sauce
* ½ teaspoon powdered sweetener
* salt and pepper, to taste

Beef it up

Preheat the oven to 400°F. Spread the bread over a baking pan, spray with low-fat cooking spray, and bake for 8—10 minutes, or until golden brown. Meanwhile, put the beans and broccoli in the top of a steamer, cover, and set over a saucepan of simmering water. Steam for 3—5 minutes, or until tender. Cool under cold running water.

To make the dressing, put the yogurt, tomato paste, Worcestershire sauce, and sweetener in a bowl, then season lightly with salt and pepper.

Preheat a ridged grill pan over high heat. Spray the steaks with low-fat cooking spray, then season with salt and pepper. Cook in the hot pan for 2 minutes on each side for medium—rare, 3 minutes for medium, and 4 minutes for well done. Transfer to a plate for a few minutes. Put the lettuce, cucumber, and steamed vegetables in a bowl. Drizzle with the dressing and toss. Sprinkle with the croutons. Divide the salad among four bowls. Thinly slice the steaks and arrange over the top, then serve.

Good bacteria

As fermented milk, yogurt is a natural source of probiotics, which help us to maintain a healthy digestive tract and immune system. Research has shown that they can even improve your cholesterol if eaten regularly.

Spiced chicken salad

Per serving: 257 cals 6.5g fat 1.5g sat fat 42g protein 7.5g carbs 1.5g fiber

This yogurt marinade, made with mellow Indian spices, is low in fat but full of flavor. Serve the chicken straight from the broiler over the cool, crisp salad greens for the best result.

Serves 4

* 3 ounces mixed mustard greens, such as red coral leaf, mustard, and red mustard greens
* 4 ounces mixed lettuce leaves
* ½ cucumber, thinly sliced
* ½ cup coarsely chopped fresh cilantro

Spiced chicken

* 1 cup low-fat plain yogurt
* 1 teaspoon cumin seeds, coarsely crushed
* 1 teaspoon garam masala
* ½ teaspoon turmeric
* 1 garlic clove, finely chopped
* 2 tablespoons finely chopped fresh cilantro
* 1 pound skinless, boneless chicken breasts, cut into cubes
* salt and pepper, to taste

Dressing

* 1 tablespoon olive oil
* ½ teaspoon cumin seeds, coarsely crushed
* ½ teaspoon crushed red pepper flakes
* juice of 1 lemon
* ½ teaspoon powdered sweetener

Sizzle time!

To make the spiced chicken, spoon the yogurt into a bowl, add the cumin seeds, garam masala, and turmeric, then the garlic and cilantro, and season with a little salt and pepper. Stir, then add the chicken and toss gently together until the meat is evenly coated. Cover and chill in the refrigerator for 1 hour.

To make the dressing, put the oil in a skillet, sprinkle on the cumin and crushed red pepper flakes, and warm over medium heat for 1—2 minutes, or until the aroma rises up. Remove from the heat, add the lemon juice, then stir in the sweetener and let cool.

When ready to serve, put the mustard and lettuce leaves in a salad bowl. Sprinkle the cucumber and cilantro over the top. Preheat the broiler to medium—hot. Thread the chicken onto eight metal skewers and broil, turning several times, for 12—15 minutes, or until browned and cooked through. Cut through the middle of a piece to check that the meat is no longer pink and any juices run clear and are piping hot. Drizzle the dressing over the salad. Slide the chicken off the skewers onto the salad.

Spiced chicken
salad
page 121

Steak salad with
light Thousand
Island dressing
page 120

Jerk turkey with tropical fruit salsa

Full of Caribbean flavor, this easy low-fat, low-calorie supper is really filling and satisfying!

Serves 4

* 1 butterhead lettuce, leaves separated and torn into bite-size pieces
* juice of 1 lime
* 1 small pineapple, trimmed, peeled, quartered, cored, and cut into thin wedges
* 1 pound turkey breast slices
* 2 tablespoons sherry vinegar
* 1 tablespoon tomato paste
* leaves from 3 stems of fresh thyme
* little low-fat cooking spray
* salt and pepper, to taste

Salsa

* 1 small mango, halved, pitted, peeled, and diced
* 1 small red bell pepper, halved, seeded, and chopped
* 2 scallions, finely chopped
* finely grated zest of 1 lime and juice of ½ lime

Jerk rub

* 1 teaspoon ground allspice
* 1 teaspoon paprika
* 1 teaspoon crushed red pepper flakes
* juice of ½ lime

How to make it

To make the salsa, put the mango, red bell pepper, and scallions in a bowl, then stir in the lime zest and juice and season with a little salt and pepper.

Put the lettuce in a large shallow bowl, sprinkle with the juice of one lime and a little salt and pepper, and toss.

To make the jerk rub, put the allspice, paprika, red pepper flakes, and a pinch of salt in a bowl. Add the juice of half a lime and mix.

Preheat the broiler to hot. Arrange the pineapple in a single layer in a baking pan and sprinkle with a little of the jerk rub. Broil for 2—3 minutes, until just beginning to brown. Transfer to a plate.

Arrange the turkey slices on the broiler rack. Add the sherry vinegar, tomato paste, and thyme leaves to the jerk rub, then spread over the turkey. Spray with cooking spray, then broil for 12—15 minutes, turning and brushing with the pan juices once, until browned and cooked through. Cut through the middle of a slice to check that the meat is no longer pink and any juices run clear and are piping hot. Cut into thin strips.

Nestle the warm pineapple in the lettuce leaves, pile the turkey on top, then spoon the salsa over it and serve on four plates.

Per serving: 217 cals   2.2g fat   0.5g sat fat   28.3g protein   22g carbs   3.3g fiber

Chicken cobb salad

Per serving: 270 cals   14.6g fat   4.7g sat fat   27g protein   8.2g carbs   4g fiber

A classic salad made low calorie with a lovely and light dressing — perfect for lunch or an appetizer if you're planning a healthy meal for friends.

Serves 4

* 2 eggs
* little low-fat cooking spray
* 4 strips of turkey bacon, diced
* 2 romaine lettuces, leaves separated and cut into bite-size pieces
* 2 tomatoes, cut into wedges
* 1⅔ cups diced, cooked skinless, boneless chicken breast
* ⅓ cup crumbled blue cheese

Dressing

* 2 tablespoons balsamic vinegar
* 1 teaspoon Dijon mustard
* 2 tablespoons olive oil
* ¼ teaspoon salt
* ¼ teaspoon pepper

It's chicken time!

To make the dressing, put all the ingredients in a bowl and whisk together.

Put the eggs in a saucepan and pour in enough cold water to cover them by ½ inch. Bring to a boil, then reduce the heat and boil for 8 minutes. Drain immediately, cool quickly under cold running water, then peel, discard the yolks, and chop the whites.

Place a skillet sprayed with low-fat cooking spray over medium—high heat. Add the bacon and cook for 2—3 minutes, or until lightly colored, crisp, and cooked through.

Put the lettuce and tomatoes in a bowl and toss gently together. Drizzle enough dressing over the salad to coat. Divide the salad among four plates and top with the chicken, bacon, cheese, and egg whites. Drizzle with the remaining dressing and serve immediately.

Vietnamese shredded chicken salad

Per serving: 267 cals 7g fat 2g sat fat 37g protein 13.8g carbs 3.8g fiber

This salad is dressed with a concentrated homemade chicken stock mixed with zingy lime juice, instead of an oil-based vinaigrette, for a fresh-tasting dish that's low in fat and carbs.

Serves 4

* 2 carrots
* 1 zucchini
* 1½ cups ready-to-eat bean sprouts
* 2 Bibb or Boston lettuces thickly sliced
* ½ cup coarsely chopped fresh cilantro

Chicken

* 2¼-pound ready-to-cook whole chicken
* 2 lemon grass stalks, halved lengthwise
* 1 celery stalk, sliced
* 1 onion, quartered
* 2 carrots, sliced
* 5 cups cold water
* 2 tablespoons soy sauce

Dressing

* finely grated zest and juice of ½ lime
* 1 red chile, seeded and finely chopped
* 2 teaspoons Thai fish sauce

Time to get started

To cook the chicken, put it, breast side down, in a deep saucepan only a little bigger than the bird. Add the lemon grass, celery, onion, and carrots. Pour in the water, ensuring it covers the bird, and add the soy sauce. Bring to a boil, cover, and simmer for 1 hour, or until cooked through. Lift the chicken out of the pan. Pierce the thickest part of the leg between the drumstick and thigh with the tip of a sharp knife; any juices should be piping hot and clear, with no traces of pink. Cover and let cool. Boil the stock for 30—45 minutes, until reduced down to 1 cup. Strain into a gravy separator and let cool.

Shave the carrots and zucchini into long, thin ribbons, using a swivel-blade vegetable peeler, and put them in a bowl. Add the bean sprouts, lettuce, and cilantro and toss.

To make the dressing, strain the fat off the chicken stock, then measure out ⅔ cup of the liquid and pour it into a large bowl. Add the lime zest and juice, chile, and fish sauce and mix. Take the meat off the chicken, shred it into thin strips (discarding the skin and bones), and add it to the dressing, then toss together. Spoon the salad onto four plates, top with the chicken, and serve.

Chicken for calorie counters

Although chicken meat is low in calories, discard the skin if you are watching your calorie intake, and skim the fat from homemade stock to keep fat levels low.

Asian tuna & wild rice salad

Per serving: 334 cals   0.8g fat   0.1g sat fat   21g protein   60g carbs   2.9g fiber

This filling rice salad is a healthy mix of high-fiber wild rice, protein-rich tuna, and crunchy vegetables, tossed in an oil-free soy and ginger dressing.

Serves 4

* ⅓ cup wild rice
* 1 cup long-grain white rice
* ¼ cucumber, diced
* 1 cup quartered button mushrooms
* ½ cup coarsely chopped fresh cilantro
* 1 (5-ounce) can chunk light tuna in natural spring water, drained and flaked
* 8 asparagus spears, trimmed
* ½ cup thinly sliced snow peas

Dressing

* finely grated zest and juice of 1 lime
* ¾-inch piece of fresh ginger, peeled and finely grated
* 3 tablespoons light soy sauce
* 2 tablespoons sweet chili dipping sauce

How to make it

Put the wild rice in a saucepan of boiling water. Bring back to a boil, then simmer, uncovered, for 10 minutes. Add the white rice and cook for 8—10 minutes, or according to the times in the package directions, until all the grains are tender. Drain, rinse, drain again, then transfer to a salad bowl.

Add the cucumber, mushrooms, and cilantro, toss gently together, then scatter on the tuna.

To make the dressing, put all the ingredients in a small bowl, then whisk until smooth. Drizzle the dressing over the salad and toss gently together.

Lay a spear of asparagus on a cutting board, then shave it into long, thin ribbons, using a swivel-blade vegetable peeler. Continue until all the spears have been sliced.

Divide the salad among four plates. Top with the asparagus and snow peas and serve.

Smoked salmon & asparagus salad with crab dressing

Per serving: 135 cals 3.7g fat 0.8g sat fat 19.5g protein 7g carbs 3.4g fiber

This luxurious salad is superquick to prepare and will leave your friends really impressed. Use fresh or frozen crab if possible, but if you can't find it in the supermarket, cheat and use canned.

Serves 4

* 16 asparagus spears, trimmed
* 1 butterhead lettuce, leaves separated and torn into bite-size pieces
* 1 red-tinged Bibb or lollo rosso lettuce, leaves separated and torn into bite-size pieces
* 7 ounces sliced smoked salmon, cut into strips
* 4½ ounces white cooked crabmeat
* pinch of paprika, to garnish

Dressing

* 2 tablespoons low-fat sour cream
* 2 tablespoons dark cooked crabmeat
* pinch of ground mace (optional)
* juice of 1 lemon
* salt and pepper, to taste

Toss it together

Put the asparagus in the top of a steamer, cover, and set over a saucepan of simmering water. Steam for 4–5 minutes, or until tender. Let cool.

Put all the lettuce leaves in a salad bowl. Top with the smoked salmon, then sprinkle with the white crabmeat.

To make the dressing, put the sour cream, dark crabmeat, and mace, if using, in a small bowl. Whisk together until smooth, then gradually mix in the lemon juice and season with a little salt and pepper.

Divide the salad among four plates. Top with the asparagus, then drizzle with the dressing and garnish with the paprika.

Selenium for fertility

Crab and other shellfish are good sources of the trace mineral selenium, which works with vitamin E for normal growth and fertility, good liver function, and hormone production. As an antioxidant, it is believed to help offset the effects of oxidized fats, which can contribute to the growth of cancerous tumors.

Super light salad Niçoise

A classic French salad, made with a reduced-oil dressing to keep the calories down and topped with melt-in-the-mouth slices of grilled fresh tuna and dainty quail eggs. It's higher in calories than most recipes in this chapter, but is included because it is filling enough to be a hearty main course.

Serves 4

* 14 ounces baby new potatoes, thickly sliced
* 2 cups broccoli florets and sliced stems
* 1½ cups halved green beans
* 2 romaine lettuce hearts, leaves separated and larger ones shredded
* 3 tomatoes, diced
* ½ cucumber, halved lengthwise, seeded, and diced
* ½ red onion, thinly sliced
* ¾ cup stoned black ripe olives
* 2 tablespoons coarsely chopped fresh flat-leaf parsley
* 12 quail eggs
* 2 (8-ounce) tuna steaks
* little low-fat cooking spray
* salt and pepper, to taste

Dressing

* juice of 1 lemon
* 2 tablespoons olive oil
* 3 tablespoons balsamic vinegar

Create your salad

Put the potatoes in the top of a steamer, cover, and set over a saucepan of simmering water. Steam for 6–8 minutes, or until tender. Lift off the steamer and let cool. Add the broccoli and beans to the simmering water and cook for 2 minutes, or until just tender, then drain and let cool.

To make the dressing, put the lemon juice, oil, and vinegar in a screw-top jar, season with a little salt and pepper, screw on the lid, and shake well.

Put the lettuce in a salad bowl, then top with the tomatoes, cucumber, red onion, olives, and parsley. Add the potatoes, broccoli, and green beans. Drizzle the dressing over the salad and toss gently together.

Cook the quail eggs according to the package directions. Drain and rinse with cold water. Preheat a ridged grill pan over high heat. Spray the tuna with low-fat cooking spray, season with salt and pepper, and cook for 1½ minutes on each side for rare or 2½ minutes on each side for medium, using more spray if needed. Cut into thin slices.

Divide the salad among four plates. Peel some of the quail eggs and leave others with their shells on, then cut them in half. Nestle them in the salads, top with the tuna, and serve.

Per serving: 387 cals   13.8g fat   2.6g sat fat   33.7g protein   33.9g carbs   8g fiber

Asian tuna
& wild rice salad

page 128

Smoked salmon
& asparagus
salad with crab
dressing

page 129

Shrimp taco salad

Per serving: 226 cals 9g fat 1.3g sat fat 19.6g protein 19.5g carbs 5g fiber

Make tortillas go farther by cutting them into thin strips and tossing them in your salad. They contrast wonderfully with crisp lettuce leaves and fresh shrimp.

Serves 4

* 2 corn tortillas
* little low-fat cooking spray
* 1 small head romaine lettuce, chopped
* 1 cucumber, thinly sliced
* 1 cup frozen corn kernels, thawed
* 2 tomatoes, cut into half wedges
* 1 pound cooked, peeled shrimp, thawed if frozen

Dressing

* 2 tablespoons olive oil
* 2 tablespoons lime juice
* 1 garlic clove, finely chopped
* ½ teaspoon ground cumin
* 1 tablespoon finely chopped red onion
* 1 tablespoon finely chopped fresh cilantro
* ½ teaspoon salt

Time to get started

Preheat the oven to 400°F. Line a baking pan with aluminum foil.

Spray the tortillas on both sides with low-fat cooking spray. Cut them in half, then cut the halves into ¼-inch-wide strips. Put the strips on the baking pan in a single layer and bake for 10 minutes, or until crisp and lightly browned. Let cool in the pan.

To make the dressing, put the oil, lime juice, garlic, cumin, and salt in a bowl and whisk together until emulsified. Stir in the red onion and cilantro.

Put the lettuce, cucumber, corn, and tomatoes in a salad bowl and toss gently together. Add several spoonfuls of the dressing and toss again. Divide the salad among four plates. Top with the cooked shrimp and drizzle with the remaining dressing. Garnish with the tortillas and serve immediately.

Power shrimp

Shrimp are low in calories and an excellent source of the antioxidant mineral selenium and of the antioxidant and anti-inflammatory nutrient astaxanthin.

Bean salad with feta

Per serving: 249 cals 21g fat 5.1g sat fat 5.1g protein 11.8g carbs 3.6g fiber

A little soft feta goes a long way in this salad, adding salty seasoning to the crunchy beans and radishes and the sweet tomatoes.

Serves 4

* 3½ cups trimmed green beans
* 1 red onion, finely chopped
* 3 tablespoons finely chopped fresh cilantro
* 2 radishes, thinly sliced
* ½ cup crumbled feta cheese
* 1 teaspoon finely chopped fresh oregano or ½ teaspoon dried oregano
* 2 tablespoons red wine vinegar
* ⅓ cup extra virgin olive oil
* 2 tomatoes, cut into wedges
* pepper, to taste

To make this salad

Put the beans in a saucepan of boiling water. Bring back to a boil, then simmer for 5 minutes, or until tender. Drain, rinse with cold water, then drain again. Cut them in half and transfer them to a salad bowl. Add the red onion, cilantro, radishes, and feta.

Sprinkle the oregano over the salad, then season with pepper.

To make the dressing, put the vinegar and oil in a bowl and whisk. Drizzle the dressing over the salad, add the tomatoes, toss gently together, and serve.

Great green beans

Tender and slender, green beans are a good source of micronutrients, minerals, and vitamins. Plus, they are cholesterol-free, rich in dietary fiber for good colon health, and rich in soluble fiber to help slow down the metabolism of carbohydrate, which regulates blood sugar levels.

Vegetable confetti with omelet spirals

Per serving: 378 cals 12.6g fat 3.4g sat fat 16.8g protein 48g carbs 6.6g fiber

For a filling salad that's fairly low in calories, look no farther than this colorful treat. The vegetables keep well in the refrigerator, so it's a good stand-by meal for after work.

Serves 4

* 3¾ cups vegetable stock
* 1⅓ cups quinoa
* 1 zucchini, coarsely grated
* 1 carrot, coarsely grated
* 3 small raw beets, green stem trimmed, coarsely grated

Dressing

* finely grated zest and juice of 1 unwaxed lemon
* 2 tablespoons light soy sauce
* ½ cup finely chopped fresh cilantro
* pepper, to taste

Omelet

* 4 eggs
* 1 small red chile, seeded and finely chopped
* 2 tablespoons coarsely chopped fresh cilantro
* 2 tablespoons water
* 2 teaspoon sunflower oil

For something "eggstra" special ...

Bring the stock to a boil in a saucepan, add the quinoa, and simmer for 10—12 minutes, until the germs separate from the seeds. Drain off the stock and discard, and spoon the quinoa into a salad bowl. Let cool.

To make the dressing, put the lemon zest and juice and soy sauce in a small bowl and whisk together. Add the cilantro, season with a little pepper, and stir.

Add the zucchini, carrot, and beets to the quinoa. Drizzle the dressing over the salad and toss gently together.

To make the omelet, crack the eggs into a bowl, add the chile, cilantro, and water, season with pepper, and whisk. Heat 1 teaspoon of the oil in a skillet over medium heat. Pour in half the egg mixture and cook, moving the softly set egg in folds toward the center of the pan, for 4—5 minutes, until the underside is golden and the egg is just set. Loosen the edges, slide the omelet onto a board, roll it up, then let cool for 5 minutes. Make a second omelet in the same way. Thinly slice and arrange over the salad.

Carrots

Carrots are rich in beta-carotene, which is converted by the body into vitamin A. This nourishes the skin and helps to keep wrinkles at bay. The soluble fiber carrots contain helps lower cholesterol and the carotenoids may lower the risk of heart disease.

Reduced-calorie potato salad

Per serving: 145 cals   0.8g fat   0.4g sat fat   5.1g protein   29g carbs   4.3g fiber

Watching your weight doesn't mean you have to give up potato salads. Simply replace calorie-laden mayonnaise with a healthier virtually fat-free yogurt-and-herb dressing.

Serves 4

* 1½ pounds baby new potatoes, thickly sliced
* 1 cup arugula

Dressing

* ⅔ cup low-fat plain yogurt
* 1 teaspoon Dijon mustard
* ½ teaspoon powdered sweetener
* 2 scallions, finely chopped
* ¼ cup coarsely chopped fresh dill
* 1 cup finely chopped fresh flat-leaf parsley
* salt and pepper, to taste

Steam power

Bring out the full flavor of new potatoes by steaming instead of boiling them. Steamed potatoes taste better, and the vitamin C found in the skins is not lost in the cooking water. Potatoes also contain the B vitamins and fiber, but are best known as a source of energy-boosting complex carbohydrates. They are low in fat and contain small amounts of protein.

Toss it together

Put the potatoes in the top of a steamer, cover, and set over a saucepan of simmering water. Steam for 6—8 minutes, or until tender. Lift off the steamer and let cool for 10 minutes.

Meanwhile, to make the dressing, put the yogurt in a large bowl. Add the mustard and sweetener and stir well. Add the scallions, dill, and parsley, season well with salt and pepper, and stir again.

Add the warm potatoes to the dressing and toss gently together, then let cool completely. Spoon into four bowls, top with the arugula and serve.

Spinach, zucchini & mint salad

Per serving: 75 calories 1.3g fat 0.5g sat fat 5.9g protein 11.8g carbs 3.6g fiber

A light, fresh zucchini-base salad bathed in a superhealthy, low-fat dressing made with plain yogurt.

Serves 4

* 2 zucchini, cut into batons
* 1 cup green bean pieces (cut into thirds)
* 1 green bell pepper, halved, seeded, and cut into strips
* 2 celery stalks, sliced
* 7 cups baby spinach

Dressing

* 1 cup low-fat plain yogurt
* 1 garlic clove, finely chopped
* 2 tablespoons coarsely chopped fresh mint
* pepper, to taste

Time to get started

Put the zucchini and beans in a saucepan of boiling water. Bring back to a boil, then simmer for 5 minutes, or until just tender. Drain into a colander, rinse with cold water, then drain again. Transfer to a salad bowl and let cool.

Add the green bell pepper, celery, and spinach, tearing any larger leaves into bite-size pieces.

To make the dressing, put the yogurt, garlic, and mint in a bowl. Season with pepper. Drizzle the dressing onto the salad and serve immediately.

Spinach for strength

Just 3½ cups of spinach per day provides 25 percent of the iron we need. There's plenty of soluble fiber in it, too, as well as vitamins A, B6, and C, potassium, manganese, magnesium, copper, and zinc. It's a rich source of omega-3 fatty acids, too, making it an all-round nutrition powerhouse.

Broccoli

Health organizations rave about broccoli as a must-have food for two powerful phytochemicals: indoles and the isothiocyanate "sulforaphane," thought to increase a group of enzymes that help fight cancer-causing agents, particularly in the prostate gland. Broccoli is also a good source of the antioxidant vitamins beta-carotene and vitamin C; the darker the florets, the more of these vitamins they contain. Steam instead of boiling it to retain as much vitamin C as you can. Broccoli contains folic acid, which is essential for moms-to-be, iron, and potassium. For those who do not eat dairy, broccoli can be a valuable source of calcium, and the soluble fiber it contains helps draw cholesterol out of your body. So keep on encouraging the family to eat more broccoli.

Green salad with yogurt dressing

Per serving: 122 cals 7.6g fat 1.3g sat fat 3.8g protein 10.7g carbs 2.3g fiber

This colorful green salad is a perfect low-calorie lunch
and a great accompaniment for meat or fish.

Serves 4

* ½ cucumber, thinly sliced
* 6 scallions, finely chopped
* 1 tomato, sliced
* 1 yellow bell pepper, halved, seeded, and cut into strips
* 2 celery stalks, thinly sliced
* 4 radishes, thinly sliced
* 3 cups arugula

Dressing

* 2 tablespoons lemon juice
* 1 garlic clove, crushed
* ⅔ cup low-fat plain yogurt
* 2 tablespoons olive oil
* salt and pepper, to taste

To make this salad

Put the cucumber, scallions, tomato, yellow bell pepper, celery, radishes, and arugula in a salad bowl.

To make the dressing, put the lemon juice, garlic, yogurt, and olive oil in a bowl and stir well. Season with salt and pepper.

Drizzle the dressing over the salad and toss gently together, then serve immediately.

Arugula power

Arugula is rich in folic acid, vitamin A and the B vitamins. It is also a good source of vitamin K. There are minerals, too, including iron, manganese, potassium, calcium, and phosphorus.

Three-bean salad

Per serving: 290 cals   16.8g fat   5.8g sat fat   12.3g protein   23.5g carbs   7.2g fiber

A small handful of cashew nuts and a little feta cheese give this filling bean salad crunch and creaminess — delicious.

Serves 4

* 3 cups mixed salad greens, such as spinach, arugula, and curly endive
* ½ red onion, thinly sliced and halved to make semicircles
* 10 radishes, thinly sliced
* 6 cherry tomatoes, halved
* ⅓ cup diced, drained cooked beets in natural juices
* 3 tablespoons dried cranberries
* ¾ cup rinsed, drained canned cannellini beans
* ½ cup rinsed, drained canned red kidney beans
* ¾ cup rinsed, drained canned great Northern beans
* ¼ cup roasted cashew nuts
* ¾ cup crumbled feta cheese

Dressing

* 2 tablespoons extra virgin olive oil
* ½ teaspoon Dijon mustard
* 1 tablespoon lemon juice
* 1 tablespoon coarsely chopped fresh cilantro
* salt and pepper, to taste

To make this salad

Put the salad greens in a salad bowl. Put the red onion, radishes, tomatoes, beets, cranberries, and all the beans in a separate bowl.

To make the dressing, put the oil, mustard, lemon juice, and cilantro in a screw-top jar, season with salt and pepper, screw on the lid, and shake well. Drizzle the dressing over the bean mixture and toss gently together. Spoon this mixture onto the salad greens.

Spoon into four bowls, sprinkle with the nuts and feta, and serve.

Go nuts for cashews

Cashew nuts have a lower fat content than most nuts, and most of their fat is unsaturated fatty acids. They have a high antioxidant content, which may be key to their heart-protective benefits.

Mediterranean wrap

Per serving: 298 cals 15.4g fat 2.5g sat fat 7.3g protein 32.3g carbs 4.5g fiber

Perfect for a packed lunch or quick treat,
this salad in a wrap is sure to be popular with all the family.

Serves 4

* 1 small zucchini, thickly sliced
* 1 red bell pepper, halved,
  seeded, and cut into chunks
* 1 tablespoon olive oil
* 4 soft flatbreads
* ⅓ cup tomato paste
* 3 cups baby spinach, shredded
* 4 artichoke hearts in oil,
  drained and quartered
* 8 sun-dried tomatoes in oil,
  drained and quartered
* 16 black ripe olives, stoned
  and halved
* 1¼ cups torn fresh basil leaves

Wrap it up

Preheat the oven to 375°F. Arrange the zucchini and bell pepper in a baking pan in a single layer, pour the oil over them, and toss together to coat. Roast for 20 minutes, or until softened and beginning to brown.

Meanwhile, spread each flatbread with a thin layer of tomato paste, then top with the spinach.

Put the roast vegetables, artichokes, sun-dried tomatoes, olives, and basil in a bowl and toss together. Divide the mixture between the flatbreads. Roll the flatbreads up tightly, slice in half, and serve.

The art of the artichoke

Globe artichokes are a good source of dietary fiber. They also contain good amounts of folic acid, the B vitamins, vitamins C and K, and minerals, such as copper, calcium, manganese, phosphorus, and iron.

Summer garden salad

Per serving: 124 cals 7.3g fat 0.5g sat fat 5.8g protein 17.8g carbs 8.3g fiber

A spicy, low-calorie tomato dressing makes a wonderful match for green beans and crisp lettuce. This salad is great on its own, or served with sliced and barbecued chicken or fish.

Serves 4

* 5 cups thinly sliced runner beans or green beans
* 3 tomatoes, diced
* 2 Bibb or Boston lettuces, leaves separated
* ½ cup finely chopped fresh mint
* ½ cup coarsely snipped fresh chives

Dressing

* 2 teaspoons olive oil
* 1 red onion, finely chopped
* 2 garlic cloves, finely chopped
* 4 tomatoes, diced
* 1 teaspoon smoked hot paprika
* 3 tablespoons sherry vinegar
* salt and pepper, to taste

Mix it up

Put the beans in a saucepan of boiling water. Bring back to a boil, then simmer for 3–4 minutes, or until just tender. Drain into a colander, rinse with cold water, then drain again and let cool.

To make the dressing, heat the oil in a saucepan over medium–low heat. Add the onion and sauté for 5 minutes, until just beginning to soften. Add the garlic, tomatoes, and paprika, then the vinegar, and season well with salt and pepper. Cover and simmer for 5 minutes, until the tomatoes are softened and saucy. Transfer to a salad bowl and let cool.

Add the beans to the dressing and toss gently together. Add the uncooked tomatoes, lettuces, mint, and chives, toss gently together, then serve.

Protective tomatoes

Vitamins A, C, and E and the minerals zinc and selenium, all found in tomatoes, can help to disarm the free radicals that are produced when the body is under stress. Lycopene, the carotene pigment that turns tomatoes red, may also help to prevent some forms of cancer by lessening the damage caused by free radicals.

Detox

Red cabbage & baby leaf salad with smoky eggplant dip

Per serving: 315 cals   16.7g fat   1.6g sat fat   7.3g protein   38.6g carbs   13.4g fiber

Give your digestive system a break with this fresh salad. Broiling eggplants until blackened all over gives this dip a wonderfully smoky flavor. Alternatively, they can be barbecued or roasted in a hot oven.

Serves 4

* 2 carrots
* 3¾ cups shredded red cabbage
* ⅓ cup raisins
* 4½ cups bistro salad (a mixture of baby red Swiss chard varieties and mâche)
* juice of 1 orange
* pepper, to taste

Dip

* 3 eggplants
* 3 garlic cloves, finely chopped
* 2 tablespoons tahini
* 3 tablespoons hemp oil

Time for a dip

To make the dip, preheat the broiler to high and remove the broiler rack. Prick both ends of each eggplant with a fork, put them in the broiler pan, and broil 2 inches away from the heat source, turning several times, for 15–20 minutes, until blackened. Let cool.

Shave the carrots into long, thin ribbons, using a swivel-blade vegetable peeler, then put them on a serving plate. Add the cabbage, then sprinkle with the raisins and salad greens. Drizzle with the orange juice and season with a little pepper.

Cut the eggplants in half and scoop the soft flesh away from the blackened skins, using a tablespoon. Finely chop the flesh, then put it in a bowl. Add the garlic, tahini, and hemp oil, season with a little pepper, and mix. Spoon into a serving bowl and nestle in the center of the salad.

Red cabbage for detox

With its intense deep purple color, red cabbage has a strong concentration of antioxidants — flavonoids that have been linked to cancer protection and indoles, thought to help reduce the risk of breast cancer by altering estrogen metabolism.

Curly endive salad with walnut oil dressing

Per serving: 200 cals 19.3g fat 2.3g sat fat 3g protein 5.7g carbs 2.3g fiber

Going on a detox can mean enjoying much simpler meals, such as this wonderful and light, crisp salad with honey-toasted walnuts.

Serves 4

* ½ curly endive, leaves separated and torn into bite-size pieces
* 1 romaine lettuce heart, leaves separated and torn into bite-size pieces

Dressing

* ½ cup walnut pieces, larger pieces broken up
* 3 tablespoons olive oil
* 1 teaspoon honey
* 1 tablespoon white wine vinegar
* 1 teaspoon Dijon mustard
* pepper, to taste

Love your lettuce

To make the dressing, put the walnuts in a skillet, add 1 tablespoon of the oil, and cook over medium heat for 2–3 minutes, or until lightly toasted. Remove from the heat, drizzle the honey over the nuts, and stir; the heat from the pan will be enough to caramelize the mixture slightly.

Add the remaining oil, stir, then let cool for 15 minutes so the walnuts flavor the oil. When it is cool, put the vinegar and mustard in a small bowl, season with a little pepper, and beat together, then stir into the walnuts and oil.

Put the curly endive and romaine lettuce in a salad bowl. Spoon the dressing over the salad, toss gently together, and serve.

Why eat walnuts?

Walnut oil is composed largely of polyunsaturated fatty acids. They are rich in protein and fiber, and provide many of the essential amino acids.

Gado gado salad

Per serving: 255 cals 17.9g fat 2.7g sat fat 10.4g protein 17.5g carbs 6.1g fiber

Tossing raw cauliflower and broccoli with crunchy bean sprouts and cucumber and coating them with an Indonesian toasted peanut and soy dressing turns everyday ingredients into something exotic and good for you.

Serves 4

* ¼ head cauliflower, cored and cut into small florets
* 1½ cups small broccoli florets
* 1 cup shredded savoy cabbage
* 1½ cups bean sprouts
* 1 cucumber, peeled, halved lengthwise, seeded, and thickly sliced
* 1 red bell pepper, halved, seeded, and finely chopped

Dressing

* 2 tablespoons peanut oil
* ¾ cup unsalted peanuts, finely chopped
* 2 garlic cloves, finely chopped
* 2 tablespoons soy sauce
* juice of 2 limes
* ½ red chile, seeded and finely chopped

Toss it together

Put the cauliflower, broccoli, cabbage, bean sprouts, cucumber, and red bell pepper in a salad bowl and toss gently together.

To make the dressing, heat 1 tablespoon of the oil in a skillet over medium heat. Add the peanuts and garlic and stir-fry for 2—3 minutes, or until lightly browned. Remove from the heat and stir in the soy sauce, lime juice, chile, and remaining oil, then let cool.

When ready to eat, spoon the dressing over the salad and toss gently together. Spoon into four bowls, then serve immediately.

Bean sprout bonanza

Popular in Chinese and Asian recipes, "mung" bean sprouts are widely available in supermarkets all year round. Low in calories, they can be added to salads in place of noodles or rice.

Rainbow salad with wasabi dressing

Per serving: 117 cals 8.8g fat 0.8g sat fat 4g protein 7.4g carbs 1.7g fiber

A salad doesn't need to be complicated to be good, it just comes down to the quality of the ingredients. This bright, healthy salad is a fun way to encourage children and adults to be more adventurous with the vegetables they eat.

Serves 4

* 1 tablespoon sunflower oil
* ¼ cup sunflower seeds
* 2 tablespoons soy sauce
* 3 cups shredded rainbow Swiss chard leaves

Dressing

* 1 teaspoon wasabi paste
* 1 tablespoon mirin
* juice of 1 small orange
* pepper, to taste

How to make it

Heat the oil in a lidded skillet over medium heat. Add the sunflower seeds, cover with the lid, and cook for 2–3 minutes, shaking the pan so they don't stick, until you hear them begin to pop. Remove the pan from the heat, add the soy sauce, cover with the lid again, and let cool.

To make the dressing, put the wasabi paste, mirin, and orange juice in a screw-top jar, season with a little pepper, screw on the lid, and shake well.

Put the chard leaves in a salad bowl. Drizzle the dressing over the salad, then toss gently together. Sprinkle on the toasted sunflower seeds and serve.

Sunflower seeds

Sunflower seeds are a useful source of vitamin E, a powerful antioxidant, and linoleic acid needed for maintenance of cell membranes. You can make extra toasted seeds and store them in a jar in the refrigerator as a snack.

Buckwheat noodle salad

Per serving: 370 cals   17.5g fat   3.4g sat fat   16g protein   40g carbs   5.9g fiber

A Japanese-inspired salad made with just-cooked soba noodles, nutrient-boosting broccoli and protein-packed edamame, tossed in a tamari and ginger dressing.

Serves 4

* 5½ ounces soba noodles
* 1⅓ cups frozen edamame (soybeans)
* 3 cups small broccoli florets and thinly sliced stems
* 1 red bell pepper, halved, seeded, and thinly sliced
* 1 purple or orange bell pepper, halved, seeded, and thinly sliced
* 2 cups thinly sliced cremini mushrooms
* 3 cups ready-to-eat sunflower sprouts or other sprouts

Dressing

* 2 tablespoons rice vinegar
* 2 tablespoons tamari (Japanese soy sauce)
* ¼ cup rice bran oil
* 1½-inch piece of fresh ginger, peeled and finely grated

Full steam ahead

Put cold water in the bottom of a steamer, bring to a boil, then add the noodles and frozen edamame and bring back to a boil. Put the broccoli in the top of the steamer, then put it on the steamer base, cover, and steam for 3–5 minutes, or until the noodles and vegetables are just tender. Drain and rinse the noodles and edamame, then drain again and transfer to a salad bowl. Add the broccoli, then let cool.

To make the dressing, put the vinegar, tamari, oil, and ginger in a screw-top jar, screw on the lid, and shake well. Drizzle the dressing over the salad and toss gently together.

Add the red and purple bell peppers and mushrooms to the salad and toss again. Spoon into four bowls, then top with the sprouts and serve immediately.

Edamame (soybeans)

Japanese edamame, or fresh soybeans, are a good source of all the essential amino acids, making them an excellent bean to eat if following a vegetarian diet. They are also a good source of the micronutrients, vitamin K, folate, manganese, and fiber. It is thought that the isoflavones they contain may mimic the female hormone estrogen, so helping with symptoms of the menopause.

Miso & tofu salad

Per serving: 204 cals 11.5g fat 1.3g sat fat 12.8g protein 14.5g carbs 4.6g fiber

Protein-rich tofu cooked in a soy, miso, and garlic glaze and served with a crisp, crunchy asparagus and bean sprout salad — superhealthy and superdelicious.

Serves 4

* 14 ounces firm tofu, drained and cut into ½-inch slices
* 1 tablespoon sesame seeds
* 1 cup thinly sliced snow peas
* 1 cup bean sprouts
* 8 asparagus spears, trimmed and cut into long, thin slices
* 1 zucchini, cut into matchsticks
* 1 Bibb or Boston lettuce, leaves separated and cut into long slices
* ½ cup coarsely chopped fresh cilantro
* 3 cups alfalfa sprouts, radish sprouts, or other sprouts

Dressing

* 3 tablespoons rice wine vinegar
* 2 tablespoons soy sauce
* 3 tablespoons sunflower oil
* 1 tablespoon sweet white miso
* 2 garlic cloves, finely chopped

How to make it

To make the dressing, put the vinegar and soy sauce in a screw-top jar, then add the oil, miso, and garlic. Screw on the lid and shake well.

Preheat the broiler to high and line the broiler pan with aluminum foil. Put the tofu on the foil in a single layer. Mark crisscross lines over each slice using a knife, then sprinkle with the sesame seeds. Spoon half the dressing over, then broil for 8—10 minutes, turning once, until browned.

Put the snow peas, bean sprouts, asparagus, zucchini, and lettuce on a plate. Pour the remaining dressing over the vegetables and toss gently together. Sprinkle with the cilantro and sprouts, then top with the hot tofu, drizzle with any pan juices, and serve immediately.

Quinoa salad with fennel & orange

Per serving: 388 cals 8.3g fat 1.9g sat fat 10g protein 54g carbs 8.4g fiber

Fennel is known to be an effective diuretic and has a calming effect on the stomach, so it is a useful addition to any detox diet. It also contains beta-carotene and folate.

Serves 4

* 3½ cups vegetable stock
* 1⅓ cups quinoa, rinsed and drained
* 3 oranges
* 1 fennel bulb, thinly sliced using a mandoline, green feathery leaves reserved and torn into small pieces
* 2 scallions, finely chopped
* ¼ cup coarsely chopped fresh flat-leaf parsley

Dressing

* juice of ½ lemon
* 3 tablespoons olive oil
* pepper, to taste

How to make it

Bring the stock to a boil in a saucepan, add the quinoa, and simmer for 10—12 minutes, or until the germs separate from the seeds. Drain off the stock and discard, then spoon the quinoa into a salad bowl and let cool.

Grate the zest from two of the oranges and put it in a screw-top jar. Cut a slice off the top and bottom of each of the three oranges, then remove the peel in thin vertical slices and discard. Cut between the membranes to remove the orange segments, then squeeze the juice from the membranes into the screw-top jar.

Add the orange segments, fennel slices, scallions, and parsley to the quinoa.

To make the dressing, add the lemon juice and oil to the screw-top jar, season with pepper, screw on the lid, and shake well. Drizzle the dressing over the salad and toss together. Garnish with the fennel leaves and serve.

Get in line for quinoa

Quinoa, pronounced "keen-wa," contains all eight essential amino acids, plus it's cholesterol-free, rich in fiber and minerals, and lower in carbs than most grains. It makes a great salad base.

Oat tabbouleh

Per serving: 348 cals 18.2g fat 3.2g sat fat 10.2g protein 37g carbs 7.4g fiber

We tend to think of oats only in oatmeal or cookies, but if you buy whole-grain oats from health food stores, often called "oat groats," they make a delicious, nutty-tasting salad base that is packed with energy-boosting complex carbs and fiber.

Serves 4

* 5 cups vegetable stock
* 1 cup oat groats
* 4 scallions, trimmed
* 16 asparagus spears, trimmed
* 1 zucchini, diagonally sliced
* ½ cup coarsely chopped fresh mint

Dressing

* grated zest and juice of
  1 unwaxed lemon
* 1 tablespoon hemp oil
* 3 tablespoons olive oil
* 1 teaspoon cumin seeds,
  finely crushed
* 1 teaspoon coriander seeds,
  finely crushed
* pepper, to taste

How to make it

Pour the stock into a saucepan, bring to a boil, then add the oats. Simmer for 25 minutes, or according to the package directions, until the oats are tender and the grains have split. Drain off the stock through a strainer and discard, then spoon the oats into a salad bowl and let cool.

To make the dressing, put the lemon zest and juice, hemp oil, olive oil, cumin seeds, and coriander seeds in a screw-top jar, season with a little pepper, screw on the lid, and shake well.

Preheat a ridged grill pan over high heat. Put the scallions, asparagus, and zucchini in a bowl, drizzle half the dressing over them, and toss together. Cook in the hot pan for 2—3 minutes, or until just softened and beginning to char, turning from time to time. Let cool, then transfer to a clean cutting board and cut into bite-size pieces.

Add the remaining dressing to the oats and stir. Add the cooled vegetables, sprinkle with the mint, and toss gently together. Spoon into four shallow bowls to serve.

Amazing asparagus

In traditional folk medicine, asparagus was used as a tonic and sedative. We know it best for its antioxidant properties; it is rich in beta-carotenes and the B vitamins, plus vitamins C and E. It is not suitable for those who have gout, because it is one of the few vegetables high in purines.

Barley & crushed bean salad

Per serving: 265 cals   15.7g fat   3.3g sat fat   7g protein   22.7g carbs   5.9g fiber

Tossed with summery vegetables, pearl barley makes a filling salad. It's packed with complex carbs and soluble fiber and is a low-GI food.

Serves 4

* 5 cups vegetable stock
* ¾ cup pearl barley
* 1 cup shelled fava beans
* 1 cup peas
* 2 scallions, quartered
* 2 stems of fresh tarragon, finely chopped
* ½ cup finely chopped fresh flat-leaf parsley
* ⅓ cup pea shoots

Dressing

* 2 tablespoons flaxseed oil
* 2 tablespoons rice bran oil
* 1 tablespoon white wine vinegar
* 1 teaspoon Dijon mustard
* 1 teaspoon coriander seeds, coarsely crushed
* ¼ teaspoon crushed red pepper flakes
* pepper, to taste

Full of beans ...

Put the stock in the base of a steamer, bring to a boil, then add the pearl barley, cover, and simmer for 20 minutes. Put the fava beans in the top of the steamer, then put it on the steamer base, cover, and steam for 5—10 minutes, or until the barley and beans are just tender.

Drain off the stock and discard, then spoon the barley into a salad bowl. Add one-third of the fava beans and raw peas. Put the remaining fava beans and peas, the scallions, tarragon, and parsley in a food processor and process until finely chopped. Add to the salad bowl.

To make the dressing, put the flaxseed oil, rice bran oil, vinegar, mustard, coriander seeds, and red pepper flakes in a screw-top jar, season with pepper, screw on the lid, and shake well. Drizzle the dressing over the salad and toss gently together, then spoon into four bowls, top with the pea shoots, and serve.

Protein boosters

Proteins are an essential constituent of virtually every cell in the body; in fact, the word comes from the Greek meaning "of prime importance." They are needed for growth and repair of body tissues, to make up enzymes and hormones, and as neurotransmitters. Unlike meat, most vegetable proteins do not contain all eight essential amino acids, so aim to mix different vegetable proteins together in one meal by serving grains and beans together.

Puy lentil & Mediterranean roasted vegetable salad

Per serving: 464 cals   21.8g fat   2.4g sat fat   17.8g protein   50g carbs   17g fiber

Lentils and whole grains are vital to any detox diet. Rich in complex carbs, fiber, protein, vitamins, and minerals, they make an inexpensive and filling base to any meal. Lentils, unlike most dried beans, don't need soaking before cooking.

Serves 4

* 2 small red bell peppers, quartered and seeded
* 2 zucchini, thickly sliced
* 2 red onions, each cut into 8 wedges
* 4 tomatoes, halved
* 3 baby eggplants, halved lengthwise
* 3 stems of fresh thyme, leaves picked
* 2 garlic cloves, finely chopped
* 3 tablespoons olive oil
* 1 cup French puy or brown lentils
* ½ cup coarsely chopped fresh flat-leaf parsley
* pepper, to taste

Dressing

* 3 tablespoons hemp oil
* 2 tablespoons balsamic vinegar
* juice of 1 lemon

Time to get started

Preheat the oven to 400°F. Arrange the bell peppers, skin side up, in a large roasting pan. Add the zucchini, red onions, tomatoes, and eggplants and arrange in a single layer.

Sprinkle the thyme and garlic over the vegetables. Season with a little pepper and drizzle with the olive oil. Roast for 30 minutes, or until the vegetables are softened and browned around the edges.

Put the lentils in a saucepan of boiling water. Bring back to a boil, then simmer for 20 minutes, or until just tender. Drain into a strainer, rinse with cold water, then drain again. Transfer to a salad bowl and let cool.

To make the dressing, put the hemp oil, balsamic vinegar, and lemon juice in a screw-top jar, season with pepper, screw on the lid, and shake well.

Drizzle the dressing over the lentils and toss gently together. Peel the skins away from the bell peppers and cut the flesh into slices, then add them to the salad. Add the remaining roasted vegetables and any pan juices, then sprinkle with the parsley and serve.

Cutting down on salt

When on a detox, you should try to avoid, or at least cut way back on, salt. Too much salt can contribute to high blood pressure, which in turn can lead to heart disease, stroke, and kidney problems. We should only consume 6 g, or around 1 teaspoon, of salt per day. Many processed foods contain more salt than you would imagine. Take the salt shaker off the table, and try to gradually cut down on the amount you use when cooking. Add spices, herbs, garlic, and vinegars as flavorings instead.

Gazpacho salad

Per serving: 140 cals   10.6g fat   1.3g sat fat   2.2g protein   10g carbs   2.5g fiber

All the flavors of this favorite Spanish soup, but in a crunchy nutrient-boosting salad, tossed in a sun-dried tomato dressing.

Serves 4

* 4 tomatoes, halved, seeded, and diced
* ⅓ cup cucumber, quartered lengthwise, seeded, and thickly sliced
* 1 celery stalk, diced
* 1 scallion, finely chopped
* ½ yellow bell pepper, seeded and diced
* little fresh basil, to garnish

Dressing

* ½ cup sun-dried tomatoes in oil, drained
* 2 tablespoons olive oil
* 1 tablespoon hemp oil
* 2 tablespoons red wine vinegar
* 1 garlic clove, finely chopped
* pinch of crushed red pepper flakes
* pepper, to taste

How to make it

Put the tomatoes, cucumber, celery, and scallion in a salad bowl, then add the yellow bell pepper and toss gently together.

To make the dressing, put the sun-dried tomatoes in a blender. Add the olive and hemp oils, then the vinegar, garlic, and red pepper flakes. Season with pepper, then process until you have a coarse paste.

Spoon the dressing over the salad, toss gently together, then garnish with the basil leaves.

Index